Finances
for the
Everyday
Family

Everyday
Finances
for the
Everyday
Family

Mike Yorkey

An Imprint of Barbour Publishing, Inc.

© 2015 by Back to the Bible.

Print ISBN 978-1-63058-368-2

eBook Editions:
Adobe Digital Edition (.epub) 978-1-63409-180-0
Kindle and MobiPocket Edition (.prc) 978-1-63409-181-7

The authors are represented by and this book is published in association with the literary agency of WordServe Literary Group, Ltd., www.wordserveliterary.com.

Published by goTandem, an imprint of Barbour Publishing, Inc., P.O. Box 719, Uhrichsville, Ohio 44683, www.barbourbooks.com

Our mission is to publish and distribute inspirational products offering exceptional value and biblical encouragement to the masses.

Member of the
Evangelical Christian
Publishers Association

Printed in the United States of America.

Dedication

To today's young families,
trying to keep their heads above water

Contents

Introduction

When it comes to everyday, kitchen table finances, I have to be honest with you: this "spending smart" business can be tough.

I don't know about you, but it seems like whenever my wife, Nicole, and I have squirreled away a little money...*blam!* We get blindsided by another big car repair bill. Or the water heater breaks. Or the property tax is due.

But that's all right. Nicole and I know God is in control—although I worry way too much. Perhaps that's because I *know* too much. I've been keeping track of the Yorkey family expenses for the last fifteen years using Quicken software, and on average we spend 97.2 percent of everything that comes in. Some years we have spent more than 100 percent—like when we had two children in college—and had to take on debt. But even in those years when we managed to spend less than we brought in, our "margin of error" was razor thin.

Life continues to be a financial scramble in our household, as I imagine it is in yours. It's my belief that today's American families—overtaxed and squeezed by stagnant pay—are barely keeping their noses above water. Many of us are living paycheck to paycheck and bracing ourselves for the next calamity—like a leaky roof or major car repair. And who knows how we're going to pay for the next car, college bills, and looming retirement.

The pressure to live within our means places tremendous stresses on everyone, but if you can spend smart on basic household expenses such as food, clothing, housing, transportation, vacations, and incidentals, you can realize a net savings of $300 to $1,000 a month. This is often the difference between a family staying financially solvent or sinking further into debt.

What expertise do I bring to the table? Well, I'm just a regular working guy—a freelance author, which means my income takes wild fluctuations year by year. I cut my teeth on spending smart when I was editor of *Focus on the Family* magazine during the 1990s. A good chunk of my workday was spent reading about and writing for families, and personal finances were as big back then as they are now. I was vitally interested in spending smart because I was earning a modest salary working for a nonprofit ministry. In addition, my wife was a homemaker, so we were living off one income.

Our family's toughest moments came when I left *Focus on the Family* magazine and uprooted my family from Colorado Springs to my hometown of San Diego. My parents still lived there, and I missed the mild Mediterranean climate of my youth. Within four months at my new job, however, the paychecks stopped. I didn't know what to do.

We were in the middle of purchasing a new home.

Mortgage lenders prefer making home loans to people who are gainfully employed. Since there was the promise of "we'll get you caught up" at my work, I continued to show up at my new job, figuring that if I helped turn around the company, then I had a better chance to receive back pay.

Meanwhile I closed escrow and took out a first trust deed for $15,000 more to tide us through the tough times. I worked four and a half months without a paycheck before finally deciding that I could no longer contribute to a fantasy world where the employees worked for free. I found a cubbyhole at home and started my freelance writing career.

Looking back, the only way we made it was by the grace of God and His people, who financially blessed us in miraculous and incredible ways. We also had a dogged determination not to take on any debt besides our home mortgage. That meant keeping an aging Mercury Villager minivan and driving a well-used Toyota Tercel that I paid $2,500 for. We also made sure we paid off our credit card statements in full each month, which was a miracle in itself.

We've since righted the financial ship in our family, but looking toward the horizon, I'd say that times are tougher today for American families. For sure, there are black clouds looming offshore—threatening clouds that first appeared during the start of the Great Recession in 2008. My sense is that gale-force winds are drawing closer to shore.

The evidence is swirling around us. The shrinking middle

class is being squeezed every day. With food prices mounting, high gas prices here to stay, and heating and electrical bills poised to skyrocket due to government regulation from perceived climate change, American families feel like they're caught outside in an unexpected snowstorm—without warm jackets.

As part of compiling this book, I surveyed 125 Christian families on their finances about spending smart. Sixty-seven percent said they were struggling to keep their noses above the water line, adding that the pressure to live within their means placed a tremendous stress on their marriages, causing dissention and even leading to divorce in some instances. Many couples said they were looking for new ways to save on basic household expenses such as food, clothing, and transportation.

If that tall order wasn't enough, these Christian families also told me that they were committed to supporting their local church, which often meant giving a significant chunk of income—10 percent in many households. These same families also supported missionaries to foreign lands, adopted a child through various Christian agencies, or gave generously to parachurch organizations like Focus on the Family.

The couples I surveyed were generous: 85 percent said they gave at least 9 percent of their income to their local churches and charitable organizations. Compare this to the national average of 2.5 percent, according to the Christian research organization Empty Tomb. With all this sacrificial giving, many who follow Christ live even closer to the edge of financial difficulties than the typical family.

Thank goodness we enjoy a priceless advantage being God's children, which means we can go to Him with our finances. He knows *exactly* where we are, and He knows our needs before we do, which brings me to the most important point of this book: *whenever you have an important buying decision, pray about it*. Just as God can direct you to a dependable used car that won't break down every other month, He can also help you find a much-needed pair of soccer shoes at a garage sale.

No Need to Worry

In one of the most comforting passages of Scripture, Jesus says, "That is why I tell you not to worry about everyday life—whether you have enough food or drink, or enough clothes to wear. Isn't life more than food, and your body more than clothing? Look at the birds! They don't plant or harvest or store food in barns, for your heavenly Father feeds them. And aren't you far more valuable to him than they are?" (Matthew 6:25–26 NLT).

Although the Lord instructs us not to worry, it's human nature to be concerned about making it to the end of the month without dipping into a dwindling savings account. Our consumerist society constantly contributes to that concern.

Blitzed with "Huge Sale!" advertisements everywhere we turn, we must be on guard against the formidable pressure to buy something.

We also face an extraordinary number of choices for *where* we can spend our money. Seventy-five years ago, our great-grandparents grew up in towns with one market, one hardware store, and one gas station. That started changing rapidly in the 1950s, and these days, behemoth "supercenters," massive modern supermarkets, expansive warehouse clubs, and niche grocery stores have sprung up in the suburbs like mushrooms.

Our great-grandparents shopped at a local five-and-dime store; we can choose from Walmart, Target, Sears, Kohl's, and Kmart. They had one clothing store; we have Marshalls, Ross Dress for Less, and T.J. Maxx. They had seasonal sales; we have digital coupons from Michael's and Bed, Bath and Beyond flooding our inboxes. They had a Sears catalog; we have instantaneous online shopping available 24/7 with Sunday delivery possible. They had mail-order companies; we have Amazon.com. They paid with cash; we carry multiple credit cards.

With all these options, how do we keep our heads and spend wisely? How do we know what is a good deal and what is not? This book will help you answer these questions, plus I'll give you lots of practical tips on stretching your spending dollars. My advice comes from research, interviews, and the

125 surveys I received from Christian families—people like you and me who are trying to stay afloat.

Allow me to explain one additional reason why I'm writing this book. It's my belief that many moms want to stay home and raise their kids. *Everyday Finances for the Everyday Family* is chock-full of ideas to help you do that. Since families can do little to save on housing and taxes, the best chance to reduce costs involves so-called "discretionary spending." This is where stay-at-home moms can make a difference. I've seen my wife, Nicole, make a huge difference in this area. We rarely go out to eat because she cooks delicious meals at a fraction of what it would cost to go to a restaurant or even "fast casual" places like Chipotle Mexican Grill or Panera Bread.

Searching out good deals on groceries and clothing—which takes time—can become a part-time job for stay-at-home moms. When you stop and figure out what it costs to send Mom back to the workforce, most families net only a few hundred dollars a month after deducting the necessary child-care expenses, new work clothes, added wear and tear on a second car, and meals away from home since tired mothers are often too wiped out at the end of a long day to cook meals from scratch. Meanwhile, a mom who has the time to hunt down bargains can easily save her family hundreds of dollars each month. Some of these reasons may help justify a mother's decision to stay at home with her children.

Of course, most single moms and dads don't have the

option of staying home with their kids during the day. They face the most difficult assignment of all: providing for their family on a single salary plus any child support they can muster. The income gap between single-parent families and two-parent families is considerable. No wonder most single moms see their style of living cut in half after a divorce.

Everyday Finances for the Everyday Family is written for all families, no matter their situation. We can all benefit from spending less than we take in by making smart buying decisions. Nearly two hundred years ago, Charles Dickens wrote this in his book *David Copperfield*:

> *Annual income: 20 pounds*
> *Annual expenditure: 19.6 pounds*
> *Result: happiness*
> *Annual income: 20 pounds*
> *Annual expenditure: 20.6 pounds*
> *Result: misery*

What a reminder that spending less money than you have in your pocket equals happiness while spending more than you take in equals misery.

But you may say, "Wait a minute. I don't feel miserable at all. I can afford these things. It's okay to have a little debt."

Yes, thanks to the ubiquitous credit card, you can afford to buy almost anything your heart desires, from a shiny new car (some dealers take Visa or MasterCard if you'll pay the 1.5 to 3 percent merchant fee) to a Caribbean vacation or a night on the town. Those purchases make us happy, and I've enjoyed those material things as well. But if you're not careful about the way you swipe your credit card in a card reader, you could become very miserable someday and not be able to spend your way out of your misery.

What's Ahead

In the coming pages, you'll discover that I've written *Everyday Finances for the Everyday Family* in a way that will arm you with sufficient knowledge to be a good shopper and save money where you can. As a writer who has written a lot of books aimed at families, I understand that today's harried parents have little patience for long-winded explanations of debt service or no-load stock funds. I think you instead want to hear concrete, tangible advice on spending your money wisely.

One thing you should know right from the beginning: I am not a tightwad. You won't find advice on how to cut up old shower curtains and turn them into baby bibs or how to collect clothes dryer lint to make your own stuffed animals. Rather, my goal is to help you save a few dollars here and there on everyday family purchases, which can help you stay out of debt and live within your means. Spend money smartly.

But there's another aspect to keep in mind. Saving

money on household items may allow you and your family to support that missionary family on furlough you met or let you financially respond when your church announces a building fund drive. The Lord delights in our gifts—not because He needs them but because we are faithful in supporting His work.

It's good stewardship to spend money wisely and stretch your paycheck as far as you can. The key word is *balance*. God has given us financial resources—be they limited or plentiful—and we are "to be content with whatever [we] have" (Philippians 4:11 NLT).

Final thought: if we're not smart with a little money, then we certainly won't be smart with a lot of money.

1

We Spent How Much?

When I worked at Focus on the Family in the 1990s, I was a guest speaker on saving money at the Focus on the Family Institute for Family Studies. Each semester, I stood before forty bright college students—who came to Focus's Colorado Springs campus for five months of intensive family-related classes—and told them my story.

"When Nicole and I purchased our first home in Southern California, it was a thirty-year-old tract home that needed a new roof," I began. "We did our best to fix up the place, doing all the work ourselves, but just after New Year's, I had a sinking feeling that we had been spending more than we had been earning all year long. In fact, we were down to less than $2,000 in our savings account. Unless we made a quick turnaround, we would be incurring some big-time debt. That's when I decided to go back and piece together our first year of home ownership as best I could.

"I went through all our credit card statements, our checkbook, and all the receipts we had saved. Then I put all those purchases for groceries, gas, clothes, car repairs, kids' piano lessons, sports equipment—anything I could think of—into one organized accounting system. When all was said and done, we spent $2,500 *more* than we brought in that year."

I had the students' attention after being so transparent.

"I took Nicole out to our favorite Chinese restaurant and shared what I learned," I continued. "We both agreed that changes were in order, so we began cutting back where we could and stretching our dollars. The following year, we showed a family profit, if you will, of $1,200."

The students registered mild interest at that point. "That works out to $100 a month. That's not much, folks."

Then I walked to the blackboard. "In a few months or perhaps a year or two, you will be graduating from college, getting your first job, and living on your own. Let's take a look at what that's going to cost."

In large block letters, I wrote RENT. "What are you going to have to pay for rent?" I asked the class. "We'll assume you'll have a roommate and rent a place where you have your own bedroom."

"Five hundred dollars," yelled one student.

"No way I'd live in a place that cheap," chimed in a young woman. "Nine hundred dollars."

"You're spoiled," retorted a male. "I can find a place for $700."

I still hadn't written a figure behind RENT. The class professor, Dr. Michael Rosebush, who invited me to speak to these students, jumped in.

"Class, the two-bedroom apartments you're living in off

campus cost us $2,000 a month."

A murmur swept the room. *That's $1,000 a month for each student.*

I wrote $1,000 behind RENT and moved on to groceries. Some thought they could eat for $250 a month, while others were sure they would have to spend $500. I jotted down a middle figure: $350. But I knew many of them didn't cook for themselves, so I said we had to come up with a figure for restaurant meals. We settled on another $350 a month, which covered around one $10 meal a day.

From there we spent thirty minutes filling in numbers for the rest of the categories: smartphones, car payments, utilities, clothes, car insurance, car repairs, cable TV, health insurance, haircuts, recreation, and miscellaneous.

Then I stepped over to another part of the blackboard and wrote down the monthly take-home pay for $12 an hour, $15 an hour, and $18 an hour—decent wages for someone just getting out of college.

When we compared the "outgo" with the take-home pay, incredulous looks covered the students' faces. Those making $12 an hour had no chance; those earning $15 would break even; and those earning $18 had some cushion.

"The problem is that some of you may not earn $12 an hour with your first job," I explained.

Dr. Rosebush backed me up. "In case you're wondering, class, over half the support staff here at the Institute for

Family Studies don't make more than $12 an hour."

Talk about depressing.

"Oh, one more thing is missing here," I pointed out. "We haven't even put down your tithe."

All the air was sucked out of the room.

While that little exercise was an eye-opener for the IFS students, I wondered how many families know where their financial ship is sailing. Christian financial counselors have told me that very few couples have a budget and actually follow it.

I understand why, because Nicole and I do not have a formal budget, either. Budgets are a hassle, involve a lot of time, and are no fun. Besides, how can you foresee the need to repair a sprinkler system or replace a broken dishwasher, refrigerator, and washing machine—which happened in our household in one year?

The answer is by budgeting for those repairs—putting aside money for the worst-case scenarios. With each passing year, I see how budgets provide clear financial goals, keep us from overspending, and can actually be freeing.

I've taken some intermediate steps to get there, using Quicken personal-finance software to track our expenses. Whenever we have a "bad month," we cut back in other areas or delay purchases. Our system is not "by the book," but it has worked for us.

Build in Margin

The idea behind having a budget and tracking your expenses is that these financial practices help you understand where you are. Once you have a handle on your spending, you can build some extra margin into your life.

Margin is a good thing. Going through life without margin is like being thirty minutes late for your son's basketball game because you were twenty minutes late getting out of a meeting because you were ten minutes late getting back from lunch. Going through life without financial margin is worrying whether you are one car breakdown away from maxing out your credit cards. Going through life *with* margin means establishing parameters that leave extra money at the end of the month. For some people, this could be something as simple as buying a used minivan for $15,000 instead of buying or leasing a shiny new one that costs three times as much when you drive it off the dealer lot.

Do you know where your family finances stand? How much debt you owe? You would be surprised at the number of couples who have only a vague idea regarding how much debt they're saddled with. Many couples are afraid to seek out the answer—kind of like ignoring dizzy spells and the blood you're coughing up because you don't want to find out that you have cancer.

Since I'm not an expert on budgeting, I sought out Mahlon Hetrick, president of a ministry called Christian

Financial Counseling in Fort Myers, Florida, and author of *The Money Workbook*.

Q: What's one of the biggest mistakes you see couples making with their finances?

Mahlon: I see way too many families who have no budget, no spending plan, no savings, too much credit, too much overspending, and wanting too much too soon.

Q: Hmmm, that kind of says it all. What's the first thing couples should do to introduce themselves to budgeting?

Mahlon: Proverbs 18:13 (TLB) says, "What a shame—yes, how stupid!—to decide before knowing the facts!" The first thing couples need to do is gather the facts. You need to know how much you are paying for rent or your mortgage, what your car expenses are, and all the other household expenditures. You need to know your tax situation. Often, we discover many people are overwithholding. All they're doing is giving the IRS their money to hold before it's returned to them with no interest. That's not wise.

But the biggest problem we see is a lack of discipline with credit card use. That's why they overspend.

Q: How much credit card debt are we talking about?

Mahlon: Anywhere from $15,000 to $50,000. Sometimes even more. But you know, it doesn't matter how much income a family brings in. If you overspend with a household income of $40,000, you'll overspend with a household income of $80,000.

Q: It's been estimated that only 5 percent of couples have a budget. Is that what you're seeing?

Mahlon: I sure am. Most people think they have a budget, but what we find is that people are record keepers. They don't have a budget. They keep track of what comes in and goes out. (Author's note: That sounds like me!)

Let's assume that your outgo exceeds your income by $600 a month. If I were to ask you what the problem is, you would tell me that your outgo exceeds your income.

If I were to ask you in which category you're doing well or which area you're doing poorly, you'd have no idea. You wouldn't have any idea until you have a written guideline that tells you what you can afford to spend for your level of income.

Q: So you're saying that without putting things down in writing, you can't identify what's causing the problem.

Mahlon: That's right. You see, people do not usually have a money problem. They have an ignorance problem about money matters. They have not been taught guidelines for spending in the various budget categories based on their level of income. They also have attitude problems about money— problems with pride, greed, coveting, etc. The average family spends about 110 percent of their income living beyond their means.

By God's comparison, we are not wise, since Proverbs 21:20 (TLB) tell us, "The wise man saves for the future, but the foolish man spends whatever he gets." If we lived according to this proverb, we would eliminate 95 percent of all our money problems. But we're not listening to God. People don't understand that the Bible is the best book on finances ever written. Look at Proverbs 2:1–10 to learn how to make right decisions every time.

Q: So what's the bottom line?

Mahlon: You can listen to God or listen to the world. It's your choice. God's answer will allow you to provide better for your family, save for the future, pay your bills on time, eliminate worry and frustration, and honor Him with your tithe.

Everyone wants a quick fix, but there's no such thing. Boiled down, there are only three things you can do:

1. Increase income.
2. Lower your outgo.
3. Control your future spending.

You need to make a list of ways to accomplish these things. You need to be creative and put on your thinking cap. Start by making a list of everything you will need to buy in the next month, and stick to that list. Don't carry checks or credit cards. Carry only the cash needed for that day's planned

Everyday **Finances** *for the* Everyday **Family**

spending. That helps eliminate impulse spending.

If you choose to be a good manager, God has good news for you: He will return a blessing greater than expected. "For God, who gives seed to the farmer to plant, and later on, good crops to harvest and eat, will give you more and more seed to plant and will make it grow so that you can give away more and more fruit from your harvest" (2 Corinthians 9:10 TLB).

What better thing than to bank on God's Word?

Overwhelmed and Underwater

Mahlon didn't pull any punches, did he? He says that the average family spends about 110 percent of their income, so you can get away with spending 10 percent more than you take in one year, but if you allow those extra expenditures to continue for several years, you will be overwhelmed—and underwater.

Listen, folks: families who are spending 110 percent of what they take in are not acting wisely or thinking straight. Listen to what Proverbs 21:20 (NLT) tells us: "The wise have wealth and luxury, but fools spend whatever they get." I don't know what it is, but too many folks just shrug their shoulders about spending more than they take in, figuring that's why credit cards were invented.

Keeping spending in check involves making an attitude change. I know that many women view shopping as a recreational pursuit. I understand the rationale: shopping is a diversion, and some people enjoy the "hunt." I'm all for that, but swiping credit cards, pointing an iPhone at an e-commerce reader, and ordering online have created a mindset where it really feels as if we're not paying for something with our own money.

Being a smart shopper means that it's all about using your head and saying no for a change. Don't you teach your children what *no* means? Sure you do. Parents of older children remember the battles they experienced when teaching their toddlers the meaning of this word.

"No, Caleb, don't stick that fork into the electrical outlet."

"No, Ally, don't step into the house with those muddy shoes."

"No, Luke, I don't want you to go outside without your jacket on."

And what did your kids do? They moaned and whined and didn't like being told that they shouldn't do something.

Hopefully, we've matured beyond the tantrum stage, but nonetheless, we're not listening to God's advice. The book of Proverbs gives plenty of practical instruction on the use of money, although sometimes it's advice that we would rather not hear. Quite frankly, we feel more comfortable continuing our spending ways than learning how to use money more wisely.

Proverbs reminds us to advance the cause of righteousness with money but not to squander it (10:16); be careful about borrowing (22:7); and save for the future (21:20). The first ten verses of Proverbs 2 remind us that those who listen to God's advice and obey His instructions will be given wisdom and good sense to make the right spending decisions every time.

In other words, spend smart.

God's way will allow you to get out of debt, pay your bills on time, provide for a better future for your family, eliminate worry and frustration, and honor Him with your giving back to His work.

Let me amplify on the last point. I could be wrong on this, but common sense tells me that when families are scrambling to keep the bills paid and are running up bigger and bigger credit card bills, giving to the Lord's work is one of the first things to go. People stop giving money to support their home church, missionaries to foreign countries, or children aided by groups such as Compassion International or World Vision.

If you have put a momentary pause on giving to your local church because you think you can't afford to do so, I urge you to consider this story by author and speaker Steve Arterburn, cohost of the daily talk show *New Life Live*, heard on Christian radio stations around the country.

In Steve's early years, he was quite financially irresponsible and deeply in debt. His father had taught him to tithe, but he hadn't taught Steve anything about properly managing his money or having some margin at the end of the month. So each time a paycheck arrived, Steve would write out a check for 10 percent to the church. He never dropped it into the collection bag, however; otherwise, Steve couldn't pay his bills. He says that he was so far underwater in debt that he needed an Aqua-Lung to reach the surface.

Each month, Steve would write that check and keep it right there in the checkbook, absolutely sure that he would drop it in the collection bag just as soon as God provided a miracle. That never happened, so after a few weeks had passed, Steve would tear up that tithe check. He felt horrible each time that happened, because he knew that he wouldn't be giving anything to the Lord's work that month.

Steve sincerely believed that the standard of giving was 10 percent, although he understood that many people believed that tithing was an Old Testament standard and that we were free to give what we wanted back to God. Whatever the amount, it just made sense to Steve that one-tenth was not too much to sacrifice since he believed God had given him everything he had. Thus Steve knew what he wanted to give, but he had messed up his personal finances so badly that he felt prevented from ever achieving it.

Here's what Steve decided to do about it. He determined that if he couldn't give 10 percent, he could afford at least 1 percent to support God's work. The next Sunday, Steve left behind a check for 1 percent at church, which turned out to be a liberating experience. He felt great. Now he was a giver.

Some might criticize a faith so puny that Steve felt he

could give only 1 percent. Some might say that if his faith had been stronger, he could have given 10 percent from the very beginning. But the reality was that Steve did not have the faith or the desire to turn in even one of those 10 percent checks, but he did when it came to writing out a check for 1 percent. The result? He wasn't there yet, but he was headed toward God's best.

Next, he asked God to help him find a way to double his 1 percent tithe. Before too long, Steve was writing checks out for 2 percent.

Steve's finances improved, and I don't mean that he started making more money. He just spent his money in a smarter way. He said no to some dubious purchases. Before long, 2 percent became 4 percent as he continued to double his gifts to God. And it wasn't long before 4 percent became 8 percent, and then he reached his goal of giving 10 percent back to God.

What can we learn from Steve's victory? At a time when Steve's finances were in disarray, he committed to giving God a minimum amount. One percent may not seem like much, but it was to him at the time. When Steve was faithful in that small amount, God honored that effort—just as He honored the efforts of those in the parable of the ten talents (Matthew 25:14–30).

If giving to your church has fallen by the wayside, prayerfully consider giving *something*. If it's $20 a month, so be it. You have to start somewhere.

Steve told me that he was not just committed to giving 1 percent the first time he dropped one of those checks into the purple collection bag.

"No, I was committed to 1 percent for the rest of my life," he said. "Each new level became a lifetime commitment. I can't tell you what joy it has been to give back what has been given to me. These days I love to give. I look forward to writing as big a check as possible whenever I can, but I don't think I ever would have gotten there if I had not started somewhere."

For many of us, being a smart spender means tracking our expenses so we can figure out where all our money is going. Now it's time to zero in on how all that spending gets done. The prime suspect is the credit card, a twentieth-century invention and twenty-first-century curse.

2

Gimme Credit

I have nothing against credit cards.

In fact, I'm a big fan. Life would be pretty darn inconvenient without plastic. You can't buy anything online, book a trip, reserve a rental car, or arrange a hotel room without one, unless you're willing to let PayPal dip into your bank account. Credit cards not only open up the universe of online shopping, but now your smartphone can "use" your credit card to make purchases so you don't even have to fumble for your Visa when you're in a Starbucks line.

For all the wonderful doors they open, credit cards can also take you places that you never expected to go, like Big Al's Loan Consolidators or the Law Offices of Shyster Whiplash, where their motto is "We can get rid of your credit card debt and protect you from bankruptcy."

While many folks wonder how they could live without credit cards, the charge card phenomenon has fundamentally changed the way people think about buying stuff. I don't know how this type of thinking began, but the following is the mind-set of many Americans regarding credit cards, department store cards, and consumer loans: *I see that number on my monthly credit card bill. That's the total balance I owe, but*

I don't have to pay that amount. I only have to send them a check for the minimum amount, which is conveniently printed in a box right next to the total balance figure. The minimum balance is a trifling amount. I can handle that.

I can't believe how many people think that credit card doesn't have to be paid in full every month! They cavalierly make minimum payments every thirty days as they continue spending away, heaping each additional purchase onto their growing mountain of debt. Every day they prove the construct of Christian financial counselor Ron Blue, who says that people have a tendency to spend 34 percent more when they reach for a credit card. Human nature being what it is, paying by cash or by personal check—and actually having to count out the money or handwrite the big numbers—acts as a governor on spending.

This makes sense to me, because one would not seem to be as psychologically restrained from spending when all it takes is a quick swipe of the credit card and a scribbled signature to complete a purchase.

Buy Now, Pay Later

Based on an analysis of Federal Reserve Statistics and other governmental data, the average household owes $7,087 on their credit cards, but when you look at indebted households, the number balloons to $15,191.[1] Since American families have historically added 5 percent per year to that staggering amount, this figure will surely hurdle past the $20,000 barrier before we know it.

It's obvious that most people never consider the real cost of buying now and paying later. Nor do they contemplate what Dave Ramsey, author of *The Total Money Makeover*, said about buying stuff on credit: "Too many times we buy things we don't need with money we don't have to impress people we don't like."[2]

A massive amount of credit card debt is like reliving *Groundhog Day*: you're paying over and over for books you've already read, dinners you've already eaten, and vacations you've already taken. Out-of-control credit card debt is stealing from your future to pay for the present, and that's a terrible way to go through life. Many people call it mortgaging your future.

Excuse my bluntness, but if you're still not seeing the light, then do the math—please. Who in their right mind would pay an extra 18 percent every time they made a purchase with a credit card? That's what it will cost you if you don't pay back the full amount within a year's time. Eighteen percent is the annual tariff for most credit cards, although some people with low credit scores must pay usury rates of 22 percent and 24 percent. Even if you shift balances to "low-cost" cards, all you're doing is delaying the day of reckoning, when your finances come tumbling down like a house of cards. In the game of credit cards—you versus the issuing bank—the house always wins.

Let's examine a real-life example: your refrigerator dies, so you shop around before stopping by Home Depot to pick out a new $2,500 Samsung stainless steel refrigerator with an ice and water dispenser. You reach for your trusty MasterCard because you only have $5,000 sitting in your savings account, and there's no way you're going to use half your savings to pay for a refrigerator today.

When you add a $2,500 purchase to your credit card balance, that single charge will cost you at least $366 in interest during the next year, based on 18 percent annual interest. (Actually, the amount will be a tad higher since interest is compounded.) If you don't pay off that $2,500 refrigerator in one year's time, it's going to cost hundreds of dollars more in interest with each passing year.

It's funny and somewhat sad that some folks will shop all around town to save $100 on a new refrigerator but never understand how that effort goes up in smoke when the new $2,500 charge is added to their outstanding credit card balance.

There are other tricks that the credit card issuers employ in the hope that you're napping. Did you know that the moment you charge that $2,500 refrigerator at Home Depot you start paying interest? You don't receive a grace period when you're carrying unpaid balances forward each month.

Did you know that if the $2,500 charge pushes you over your credit limit, you'll be socked with an overcharge fee, usually an amount between $25 and $50? Actually, some people do know this, which is why they open a Home Depot charge account, hoping to receive an interest-free month before the usual high interest rates kick in, but that does nothing to address the overall problem.

Furthermore, did you know that cash advances take as much as a 4 percent hit (or $40 for a $1,000 cash advance) when you receive money from an ATM machine? Were you aware that after you receive the cash advance, you'll be *immediately* subjected to a higher interest rate—usually around 20 percent—on that amount? Another irritating charge is a $5 minimum for each cash advance, which is rather steep if you want only $50 or $100. Finally, the most grating surcharge is the $50 to *close* a credit card account.

I hope the porch light is coming on, because those are the burdensome costs of credit. Since many more families do not pay their credit card statements in full every month compared to those who do (around 75 percent of American households do not pay their credit card bills in full each month),[3] the verdict is inescapable: as a culture, Americans have a tough time handling credit cards. The evidence is reflected in the fact that the percentage of families who are more than thirty days past due has topped 5 percent of all cardholders—a number that has remained stubbornly high since the Great Recession started.

Card issuers are also boosting "charge offs"—that's

industry lingo for writing off card loans that are uncollectable. Charge offs have been steadily climbing in recent years and are around 4 percent of all cardholders. In addition, a surge of deadbeats has prompted bankruptcy filings to rise.

The credit card business must be incredibly profitable to withstand a 4 percent deadbeat rate and what must be hundreds of millions of phony charges from stolen cards and stolen credit card numbers. It seems like every couple of months we hear of a business like Target announcing that hackers wormed their way into their computer systems and stole pertinent credit card information.

One practice you *must* adopt is verifying each charge, which is another reason why you should input every credit card purchase into a personal finance system like Quicken. When you review each charge, you're far more likely to spot any bogus activity.

The "Fasten Seat Belt" Sign Is On

Okay, it's roll-up-our-sleeves time—time to get serious about turning the nose of your credit card jet from an upward trajectory and toward a descent onto the terra firma of debt-free living. Like a Boeing 787 Dreamliner beginning its descent a hundred miles from the airport, it's going to take a while to sink through the altitude of debt. (For the purposes of this chapter, I will direct my advice toward those seeking to erase their credit card bills without utilizing consolidation or home equity loan strategies.)

The passenger jet analogy is a good one. You don't drop from 10,000 meters (39,000 feet) or shed $10,000 in debt very quickly. It happens incrementally over time, with two pilots—you and your spouse—at the controls, checking your instruments, gauging weather information, and not deviating from your flight plan, which has three salient points:

1. Determine how high off the ground you are. Just as there is less oxygen with each 1,000 feet of altitude, there is less financial oxygen with each $1,000 in credit card debt. I remember the time Nicole and I climbed 14,110-foot-high Pikes Peak, overlooking Colorado Springs. After six hours of hiking, Nicole developed dizzy spells at the 13,000-foot level. My wife gulped Advil and rested after every minute of hiking to counteract the effects of high altitude. It was a long, tough haul for her to reach the summit, because she could barely breathe.

Those sitting atop a mountain of high debt have an equally difficult time gasping for air. Even though it's difficult to face your financial obligations squarely, you must begin by tallying all your credit card debts. You start by looking at your monthly statement and committing to memory the figure next to "Your Total Balance," the one that's much larger than "Minimum Amount Due."

Is it a scary number? Remember, anything over an aggregate number of $2,500 is cause for alarm. Credit card debt is a slippery slope—it doesn't take much credit card spending before your legs slip out from underneath you.

2. Take a credit card holiday. There are several great reasons to stop charging and start paying by cash or personal check. For openers, it's going to be easier to get your credit card balances paid off when you're not adding to the pile each month. With steady monthly progress, you're encouraged to keep chipping away.

Another enticement to stop using credit cards is the fact that you'll receive a healthy discount on every cash purchase because you won't be paying any charge card interest. Another thought worth keeping in mind is that suddenly paying with cash shocks the system and renews your appreciation for what things really cost.

As you embark on a credit card holiday, this would be a good time to take inventory of the cards in your purse or wallet. Most households have three to five credit and charge cards. This is no sin, of course, but having too much credit available has proven to be too great a temptation for many families.

Simplify life and scale back to one card, which you can use for emergencies or the online purchases that you absolutely have to make. One way to put your card "on ice" is to drop it in a bowl of water and place it in your freezer. As for your other cards, can you cancel them? Sure you can, but canceling a credit card doesn't cancel your indebtedness.

Any "vanity" cards like Neiman Marcus or Nordstrom's charge cards must be closed out. The so-called "bennies" from a Shell Oil card (rebates on gas purchases) or a Home Depot card (an extra 10 percent for the first purchase) are come-ons that can get you into trouble.

Those benefits remind me of the casino greeter who hands you a roll of quarters the moment you stroll onto a gaming floor. Casino bosses love to hand out $10 in quarters—which you could pocket or use to stroll through the buffet line—because they've studied human nature. Ninety-seven out of one hundred people will make a beeline for the quarter slot machines, where that roll of quarters will be gone in five minutes. They know the hook is set when people reach into their pockets and play with their *own* money.

3. Start this month to pay off the lowest cards first. I love this strategy. Let's say you have a Macy's card with $338 in "hangover" charges. Your Best Buy card has $1,249—the amount left over from the purchase of a fancy flat-screen TV for the living room wall. And your Visa card has a honking $7,442 amount attached to your name. For the moment, you can allocate only $750 per month toward paying off these three bills.

In concert with a reduced spending plan, send each credit- or $250 a month. The minimum payment for the Visa charges is 2 percent, or around $148, so at least you'll receive credit for paying off some principal. Under this approach, the Macy's bill will be cleaned up in two months and the Best Buy card will take five months. With those victories boosting your confidence, you can turn your sights on wiping out that Visa balance.

If you're serious about really taking on that large Visa debt, you're going to have to work overtime or take a second job, or send your spouse back to the workforce. (If you're both working and in some serious debt, I would recommend financial counseling.) Remember: you can't be making any major purchases, taking lavish vacations, or saving for retirement when credit card interest is financially eating you alive.

Getting Serious Help

If your financial situation is clouded by multiple debts— car payments, orthodontist bills, college loans, and nagging credit card debt—then you'll want to look into Mary Hunt's Rapid Debt Repayment Plan (RDRP) on her website, www.debtproofliving.com.

I've known Mary, the founder of Cheapskate Monthly and an articulate spokesperson for getting out of debt, for twenty years, and this is the best do-it-yourself debt-repayment plan I've come across. Repayment plans can become terribly complicated and time-consuming. Mary says that unless you have a Harvard degree in finance, it's difficult to manually create your own RDRP.

For just $29 for one year's access to her website, you

can create and continually access your own Rapid Debt Repayment Plan, which automatically sorts debts by order of payoff and creates a month-by-month payment chart that you can print out and check off as you make payments toward those debts. The RDRP will also tell you the month and year that you will be debt-free, which gives you something to shoot for.

I urge you to demo Mary's Rapid Debt Repayment Plan if you think you need help. Once you see how much extra interest you'll be paying over the next several years (the RDRP displays that as well), you'll be spurred to wipe out those household debts as soon as possible.

Another good idea is to send in your payment as soon as the bill arrives. Paying early reduces your average daily balance, interest compounding, and ultimately the total amount of finance charges you pay.

Beating Them at Their Own Game

Now let me put in a good word about credit cards.

When managed right, banks and financial institutions issuing "reward cards" will *pay you* to use your card.

We've had a Citi ThankYou Rewards card for years, and we charge *everything*. Nicole and I have reaped a ton of rewards and goodies, but the only way the card works is if you pay the statement balance in full every month so that you don't occur hefty interest charges. In return, you can book free travel—airfare, hotel rooms, and the like.

I like redeeming our ThankYou points for gift cards. We have received a $100 Starbucks card for 10,000 ThankYou points and a rebate of 1 percent on our purchases. We've also ordered gift cards for Walmart, HomeGoods, T.J. Maxx, Kohl's, Bed, Bath and Beyond, CVS Pharmacy, iTunes, Chili's, and Panera Bread.

There are other rebate cards that you can check out. If you're carrying no credit card debt, have a way to charge business items, or to get reimbursed (I've been the "banker" when paying the bill at restaurants when going out with friends), rebate cards put cash or gift cards in your pocket. Sometimes you can charge big-ticket items to your credit card. When our kids attended Azusa Pacific University, a Christian college in the Los Angeles area, all the tuition bills went right to our credit card. That was a wild ride getting those charges paid each month!

Another rebate card to check is the Costco "business" card through American Express. Each year, Costco charges us $100 for an annual membership, but a year later we receive a rebate check for around $125, based on our usage. That's on top of the 1 or 2 percent rebate American Express gives us for using the card with our Costco purchases. I generally receive a little more than $100 each year on Costco grocery and gas purchases, so a rebate of more than $225 sounds pretty good to me.

We buy most of our gas at Costco because it's the smart thing to do. These days, when it comes to the car you drive, you need to spend wisely, too, as I'll discuss in the next chapter.

3

Wheels Adjustment

I worked at Focus on the Family with Bruce Peppin, who grew up in Pasadena, California, during the sixties and early seventies listening to "car songs" by the Beach Boys and Jan and Dean.

When Bruce turned twenty, he was ready for his first set of wheels. As a new Christian, Bruce wanted to make a wise purchase, but his swirling hormones also made him yearn for a cherry-red two-door that would impress the babes and take off in a blaze of burning rubber.

In quest of just the right car, Bruce was scanning the classifieds one weekend. (Note to millennials: "Classified ads" are short, small-print listings of items for sale in a special section of something called a "newspaper.") One ad set his heart pounding: "'68 Pontiac GTO, white, Hurst 4-speed stick shift, leather, mag wheels, top shape, $800."

When he laid eyes on this beauty, he fell in love. With its jacked-up rear end and wide Tiger Paws tires, the gleaming GTO screamed muscle to any onlooker. Under the hood, a 455 V-8 engine growled at the slightest touch of the accelerator.

Bruce quickly agreed to the price set by Billy, the GTO's owner. Eight hundred bucks was a considerable amount of

Mike Yorkey

money to a college kid in those days, the equivalent of $5,000 today. The following day, Billy picked up his buyer for the ride to the bank, where the transaction would be completed. Meanwhile, Bruce, a novice car buyer, aimed a few perfunctory prayers heavenward, asking the Lord for one red light after another if the car was a lemon.

From the shotgun seat, Bruce noticed the gas gauge was a little below half full. They quickly hopped on the freeway for the ten-mile jaunt to Pasadena. The throaty engine roared as Billy slammed the accelerator to the floor and merged quickly into the No. 1 lane. He kept up a steady stream of chatter.

"Your first car, huh? Oh, you're going to love this baby. Believe me, the girls will go crazy. They'll be putty in your hands. . . ."

That wasn't exactly at the top of Bruce's priority list. He glanced again at the gas gauge, which now showed one-quarter tank left. A noticeable shift. *Hmmm*, he thought. *I have a real gas hog here. God, am I making the right decision?*

They sped down the freeway off-ramp onto Pasadena's Lake Avenue. Up ahead, a pedestrian stepped into the inter-section. They were traveling a little too fast, but Billy had time to jam on the brakes. Unfortunately, a car following a little too closely skidded into the GTO, denting the rear fender.

Bruce and Billy jumped out of the car to inspect the damage. The fender was bent in a couple of places, but the damage was manageable. "It'll be okay," Billy said. "A body shop can pop that out in no time. Whaddya say we keep that appointment at the bank?"

"But. . . ," started Bruce.

"Hey, what do you have to worry about?" Billy asked, spreading his palms upward. "This is nothing. You're gonna *love* this car."

Bruce was too timid to speak up. Bruce drove a few more blocks and then turned into a gas station. The gauge was resting squarely on EMPTY. Billy jumped out and put in a dollar of premium. (Can you tell this story happened back in the day when gas cost 35 cents a gallon?)

What a cheapskate, Bruce thought. *Man, this car sure slurps up the gas.*

Billy popped the hood. From his seat, Bruce could see him pulling out the dipstick. Then he quickly put the dipstick back into the engine block and hot-footed it over to the nearby minimart. Bruce stepped out and checked the dipstick himself. It was dry as a desert bone.

Billy returned with a couple quarts of oil. "She's a little low," he explained as he poured in the oil.

Back on the road, Bruce slumped into his seat. *This is not looking good,* he thought. *But the Lord will protect me. I'm sure it's nothing.*

Back on Lake Avenue, they hadn't traveled more than a mile when the GTO started lurching. They had just enough power to get off the road before the engine quit. Billy jumped out and popped the hood. The radiator hose was twice its normal size, and steam rose everywhere.

Finally, the Lord had Bruce's attention.

"I'm not going to be able to buy this car," he announced.

"Whaddya mean?" Billy retorted. "It's probably just a minor repair."

"Maybe, but I'm not going to buy your car."

Billy slammed the hood and cussed a blue streak. They stared at each other for a long minute before Billy left to find a pay phone. He needed to call a tow truck.

"When I got back home, I was so thankful," Bruce told me later. "I felt like the Lord was saying, 'Bruce, you weren't catching on too quickly, so I needed to teach you a lesson.' I depended on God, and I felt like He closed the door that day for my own good. A couple of weeks later, I came across a guy selling a '65 Mustang, a burgundy GT model with a black vinyl roof, tach, and tuck-and-roll, all for $800. That car served me really well for five years. In fact, I ended up selling it for $1,400 because Mustangs had become a collector's item. That was an incredible lesson not to jump the gun but to be willing to wait for God's timing."

The Road Less Traveled

I wish I had learned that lesson in my twenties. The Lord could have saved me a lot of car-buying grief—and a considerable amount of money. I also grew up in Southern

California during that time, but my Achilles heel wasn't muscle cars—it was *status*. I loved sleek, boxy BMW coupes and wanted to own and drive the "ultimate driving machine."

A San Diego BMW dealership had the perfect car waiting for me, a three-year-old two-door in a model called the 2002. The white sports car came with a sunroof and dual Weber carburetors, which meant it was *fast*. The salesman told me that the Beemer could do 35 mph in first gear, 55 mph in second gear, 75 mph in third gear, and 140 in fourth, meaning that I would rarely put the car into fourth gear.

The slick salesman pumped me up, claiming that BMWs were in such high demand that they were *appreciating* in price because the new models cost so much. If I played my cards right, I would be buying an *investment*. At this point, I might have well said, "Here, put the hook in my mouth."

The cost for a three-year-old BMW 2002 at the time? The asking price was $7,300, or $28,000 in today's dollars. The salesman said he could "sharpen his pencil" and "let it go" for only $6,700. Such a deal! I didn't even bother to dicker. With a few thousand down, the car payments worked out to a few hundred dollars a month.

But then I met—and fell in love with—Nicole. When we became engaged, I knew the Beemer had to go. It had been an expensive toy. In eight months I had spent a few thousand in repairs, but the engine was still overheating. Not a good sign. It was time to unload my "investment."

Finding someone to take the BMW off my hands wasn't as easy as the salesman had promised. After two weeks, my only offer came from a foreign college student who worked me over pretty good. I sold the car for $1,400 less than I paid for it. The cost of my one-year, 10,000-mile fling with status: a cool $3,000, or the equivalent of $10,300 today.

Ouch.

A bit wiser, I turned around and bought an old Dodge Polara for $350. The nineteen-foot boat was just the money-saving ticket for our early years of marriage. Since then we've purchased a couple of new cars, but we've kept them an average of ten years and put 150,000 miles on them. These days I drive a thirteen-year-old 2002 Nissan Altima with over 130,000 miles on the odometer. Sure, the "clear coat" has peeled off the roof and front hood and I could use a new gold metallic paint job, but for Point A to Point B driving, I like a car that was paid off years ago.

My BMW story illustrates three points:

1. Cars always cost more than you think.

2. You swallow your pride when you go "down" to a cheaper car.

3. Selling and purchasing cars involves time, research, and patience.

As you look to spend money smartly, you really have to pay

attention to where you're going when it comes to cars.

Wheeling and Dealing

Perhaps you have a similar story to tell about the impertinent days of your youth. Now you're a little older and a little wiser. You've heard financial counselors say in a deep tone of voice that cars are the "second biggest purchase you'll ever make." For what cars cost these days, that's a true statement. But the truth is that autos are the biggest purchase you'll ever make of a *depreciating* asset.

Unlike homes, which generally increase in value—which is not a given these days—automobiles (especially new ones) are monetary sinkholes that are worth less with every mile and every passing day. But we need transportation and couldn't survive without ease of mobility. We drive to work, we carpool our kids, and we do our shopping by driving our cars. Unless we live in a small town or a large city with plenty of mass transit, cars are essential to everyday living.

So how can you spend smart on this "essential" of modern-day life?

1. Buy new or used cars as cheaply as you can.
2. Keep your car well maintained.
3. Shop for the best insurance deal.
4. Look for ways to drive fewer miles.

Before you make any drastic moves—since buying and selling cars involves loads of time—determine how much you're really paying for each car in your driveway. What you want to find out is a cost-per-mile figure. You begin with using Quicken to create a report for the last twelve months that adds up all your car-related expenses. All the hard costs should be entered—car payments, insurance, gas fill-ups, oil changes, repairs, and new tires.

The hidden costs, such as finance charges on a lease or bank loan plus depreciation, are more difficult to ascertain. Most people conveniently forget that new cars depreciate by 40 percent in their first three years. Instead, they see a monthly lease payment for $349 and figure the only extra is gas. They fail to add in insurance, registration fees, the tax on the lease, and dollops of depreciation.

The American Automobile Association can help you calculate those hidden costs. If you are a AAA member, drop by a local office and ask for a AAA pamphlet called *Your Driving Costs* (much of this information can also be found at various AAA websites). While noting that the costs of owning and operating a car vary widely across the United States, the pamphlet presents an excellent snapshot of how much it costs to drive a vehicle for one mile.

The per-mile cost to drive a fairly ordinary new car—we're talking a Chevrolet Cavalier LS, a Ford Taurus SEL, or a Mercury Grand Marquis LS—is 60.8 cents per mile. Put another way, this means that it costs soccer moms $6.08 to carpool the kids to a nearby game (10 miles round-trip) or $18.24 to commute each *day* to work (figuring a half hour commute of 15 miles each way). A 100-mile round-trip to a major league baseball game would cost $60, while 50 miles in errands would be half that amount—$30. At least you can be thankful that you're not driving a Mercedes, where it's estimated that the cost per mile is almost *double*—a little over $1 per mile. Those are close to taxi rates!

At 60 cents per mile, though, it costs you $760 a month (based on driving a car 15,000 miles a year) to drive a new sedan, a figure that astounds most folks, especially since we are talking about run-of-the-mill four-doors. The more popular Jeep Cherokees and Chevy Suburbans and Dodge Ram trucks are probably around 85 cents per mile because they are more expensive, slurp more gas (10 to 15 miles to the gallon city driving), and are more costly to insure because car thieves steal trendy cars.

According to AAA, the cost to drive a five-year-old used car is about 45 cents per mile. In the past, when I've totaled up everything we spent on our two well-used cars, I came up with a figure of 50 cents per mile—and we enjoyed a "good" year on the repair side!

Still, the principle is the same: driving an older automobile will free up hundreds of dollars each month. Depreciation costs are lower because older cars are worth much less, and the state and the insurance company discount annual registration and insurance fees, respectively. If the car is paid off, then you are saving on financing fees.

Stepping on the Lot

Sooner or later, cars die.

You have three options: buy new, lease, or buy used. Regarding the first option, the decision is up to you whether to buy new. My rule of thumb is if you can't pay at least half of the purchase price up front, then you should be in the used car market. As for leasing, I've never been a big fan, but it's all in the numbers. If you have a spreadsheet put out in front of you and you can see how the numbers work, then it's worth considering. Car makers often give a lot of incentives to lease cars for two or three years, but keep in mind that those thick contracts are written in their favor. Again, the numbers have to make sense.

If you've decided that a new car is too rich for your blood and you don't like "renting" cars during a three-year lease, then you're in the used car market. You definitely have to do your due diligence when buying used; otherwise you're buying someone else's problem.

You should never buy a car without having it checked by a trusted mechanic, even though it's a hassle to drive the car to his shop and pay $100 for a good look-over. Hassle yourself.

The most powerful tool you have is the Carfax Vehicle

History Report (www.carfax.com) that will give you a complete history of the auto. You enter the vehicle identification number (VIN), and up pops DMV records, previous leases, police reports, accidents, and inspection stations where odometer readings were taken. The cost is $54.99 for unlimited access and $39.99 to run one car through their data banks.

I'm afraid there is a real problem out there with wrecked cars being rebuilt and resold. These are severely damaged cars that have been "totaled" in an accident—often with fatalities—but instead of a one-way trip to the junkyard, the insurance companies make a few bucks selling the wrecks at auto auctions. It's amazing how these wrecks can be brought back to life, but they are, and unsuspecting customers are tooling around town in cars that were creamed in an accident, flooded in a hurricane, or damaged by a tornado. Always run a car title history through Carfax.

When shopping for a used car, you have four avenues to choose from. Let's take a closer look at each one:

1. The dealer lots. You know the advertising jingle: *We keep the best and wholesale the rest.* That's true to some extent, but you pay more to purchase a used car on a dealer lot even though you exit with more peace of mind. Many dealers can't take the chance of selling shoddy products because they have a reputation to protect.

Dealers have lots of "product" to sell because of leasing,

which came to the fore in the 1990s. With Detroit automakers subsidizing leases so they could keep their assembly plants humming ("Zero Percent Financing OAC"!), more and more leased cars are returning to the dealers after their twenty-four, thirty-six, or forty-eight-month leases are up. These leased cars come back with 30,000 to 45,000 to 60,000 miles— models that can be resold or released again. When the cars are returned, the dealer supposedly inspects and reconditions each used car according to a factory checklist—replacing tires, belts, brakes, and torn upholstery. These refurbished cars are then "certified" for resale and backed by limited warranties from the factory.

These developments explain why dealers are now selling more used cars than new ones—a first-ever for the industry. Another reason why dealerships like to sell used cars is because buyers don't know what they paid for the car.

What a crazy business! Savvy shoppers for new cars can order printouts from *Consumer Reports* showing the "invoice" price (what the dealer is charged by the manufacturer) and the "sticker" price (what the dealer wants you to pay). Smart buyers negotiate from the invoice price up rather than from the sticker price down.

That negotiation advantage is lost in the used car market, and to compensate you'll have to do your homework by consulting the *Kelley Blue Book* as well as *Consumer Reports* and *Edmunds*. (You can find these resources online.) Once you're confident that you know what certain models cost, it's time to visit some dealerships. Remember, you're on their territory now, and you'll run into a car salesman who does this every day for a living, so he is an expert at "controlling" the situation.

Play your cards close to the vest and explain your situation: you need to lower the cost of every mile you drive. Stay calm. You're the buyer, and there aren't *that* many people buying cars these days. Test-drive the car, testing the car for handling, engine power, and interior noise levels. It's not a bad idea to bring your spouse along who can act as a "holdout"— someone who's not quite convinced that this is the deal to make.

When you sit down at the negotiating table, steel yourself for the tricks of the trade. You'll be put on the defensive by being asked whether you are a "today buyer," someone who's serious about getting the deal done. Be careful about making the first offer; wait to hear what he has to say first. Finally, be prepared to walk when negotiations bog down.

2. Private party. The upside to buying from a private party is that you should be able to save thousands of dollars. The downside is that you really don't know what you're buying.

Nearly every city has *Recycler* or *Auto Trader* tabloids found at convenience stores, but you can find these publications online as well. Don't expect the grainy color photos to reveal much, but at least you get some idea of the car's shape.

You can gain the upper hand by doing your research of what the car is worth at market value. Often there's a large disparity between what the car is actually worth "on the street" and the inflated value inside the seller's head.

Maybe you're like me—not the confrontational type. Maybe you don't enjoy haggling over price. If you are armed with the facts, know what certain models cost, and have run the car's VIN number through Carfax.com, you can rest assured that you are in the driver's seat when it comes to making a deal.

3. Mom-and-pop lots. Every city has them—the small, independent used car lots where Rodney Dangerfield look-alikes hold sway over their dusty inventory. Buyers have to be on their toes because they're really buying these used cars "as is." I think it would be interesting to run a Carfax report on some of the cars that end up in these boneyards, but you never know. Be careful, shop well, and you might be very happy with what you drive away with.

4. Friends and family. They say you should never buy a used car from someone you know well, and I understand the rationale. A blown engine one week after a sale can blow a friendship, but the odds of that happening are not very high.

I like my chances when buying a car from friends or family: at least you're getting a fair scoop regarding the car's repair history. You're also more likely to be dealing with a Christian brother or sister, which again would raise my comfort level.

Kicking Tires

Finally, let me close this chapter with a few more observations:

SUVs are expensive. I have nothing against sports utility vehicles; in fact, many of the most attractive cars today are the SUVs from Mercedes, BMW, and Lexus. The problem is that the automakers know it, the dealers know it, and the car-buying public knows it. With high demand, you pay more.

SUVs are Detroit's cash cows, making up half of all vehicle sales in the United States but two-thirds of the profits for the Big Three automakers. While the profit margin in small four-doors is rather thin, a Ford Explorer, Edge, or Escape can pad the bottom line with thousands of extra dollars of profit. Besides being expensive to buy, SUVs are expensive to drive. You'll pay more for repairs, gasoline, and insurance.

If you need a hauler—and every family with children needs a seven-passenger car these days—buy a minivan. I know, they're not as sexy as SUVs and have suburbia written all over their front hoods, but minivans like the Honda Odyssey, Toyota Sienna, and Acura MDX will get you and the kids there in comfort and more than enough style—and one-third less money.

Make that second car a beater truck. At one time, I drove a fifteen-year-old Chevy S-10 pickup that was in great shape. Having a light truck as a second car sure came in handy when we needed to haul bikes to the bike shop, buy wood for the winter, or bring home a piece of used furniture found at a garage sale.

I even referred to my white pickup as my "truck ministry." I let friends who were moving borrow the truck on weekends. I can remember the times when I had to borrow a truck from a friend, and being able to lend it out was my way to give back.

You don't have to let your teen get his or her driver's license at sixteen years old. Our kids didn't start driving when they turned sixteen. We were going through a rough financial patch at the time, and we told the kids that we couldn't afford to pay for their insurance or get another car. They went with the program. Andrea was almost eighteen and Patrick was seventeen when they finally got their licenses. They survived high school without a car in Southern California, and yours can as well. Your insurance rates skyrocket when there are teen drivers in the family.

To mitigate their disappointment, we told the kids that we would drive them everywhere—to friends' homes after school, to birthday parties on Saturday nights, to the movies with friends—just about anywhere. It wasn't fun pulling myself off the couch at 11:30 on a Saturday night and driving a half hour to pick Andrea and her friends up at the bowling alley, but I did it and don't regret it.

There were a couple of unintended benefits to Andrea not getting her driver's license just before she turned eighteen.

We heard story after story of classmates crashing cars and getting into wrecks even though it wasn't their "fault." Not being able to drive at sixteen and seventeen freed her from that responsibility and kept her much safer.

The greatest thing about chauffeuring Andrea around, however, was that it turned out to be a great way to spend time with her and Patrick. Nicole says she wouldn't trade anything for all the mornings and afternoons she spent with Andrea and Patrick driving them to school and back. More often than not, relationship-building discussions ensued in the "captive audience" atmosphere that only a car ride can provide.

Our teenagers also helped us do errands, like shopping for food, which can be a fun way to spend smart.

4

Supermarket Sweep

Food shopping is getting more expensive every day.

Inflation is taking a toll in the checkout lane. The news is peppered with stories about the rising costs of milk and meat. Fresh fruits and vegetables are also taking a bigger bite out of the food budget. Everything that gets dropped into the shopping cart these days costs more than it did a year ago.

As families look for ways to spend smartly on food, groceries come under scrutiny because of the hefty bite they chomp out of the family budget. If you're a family of four, you probably average $800 to $1,000 a month or somewhere between $10,000 and $12,000 a year for groceries. (By "groceries," I mean all food items plus paper towels, toilet paper, diapers, aluminum foil, shoe polish, feminine hygiene products, shampoo, dog food, etc.)

Even though we're spending more and more on groceries, the good news is that food is not a fixed expense like the rent or a mortgage. Money can be saved here. To spend as wisely as you can, I recommend the following tactics:

- buy store brands
- shop the loss leaders

- stock up on sale items
- use coupons
- frequent warehouse clubs

The overall *best* strategy is to "cherry pick" from all five of these tactics. But when it comes to supermarkets, you have to see through the sell-through.

Step into a supermarket a few days before the Fourth of July, and what are you likely to see? Long banners hang from the ceiling announcing "firecracker" savings. The employees— from stocker to lead cashier—are dressed in stone-washed jeans, red cowboy shirts, boots, and straw hats. Just inside the front door, you practically trip over a patriotic display of twenty-pound bags of barbecue briquettes, boxes of canned lighter fluid, two crates of watermelons, and 7UP cases stacked in the shape of a pyramid.

Nothing is left to chance. Track lighting illuminates the fresh produce just so, while an abundance of cheery signs guide you along. The aisles are wide enough for two carts to pass each other, but not too wide: grocers want you to easily pick things off both shelves as you pass. If you shop early in the morning or late at night (many supermarkets are conveniently open twenty-four hours a day), you can practically see your reflection in the freshly waxed, white tile linoleum.

Supermarkets offer tremendous variety. You can choose from 150 kinds of cereal, two dozen brands and types of peanut butter, and ten brands of chocolate-chip cookies. You can shop several thousand different products totaling one million items in every supermarket. Everywhere the merchandise is stacked perfectly, and nothing is out of place. A paradise of food beckons you to partake liberally of its abundance—as long as you pay the cashier on your way out.

Supermarkets purposely place the produce section on one side of the 60,000-square-foot building, with the milk and other dairy products *way* over on the other side. If you're dropping in for salad and milk, you'd better have your walking shoes on. The idea is to make you pass by a lot of mouthwatering food on your way to the high-traffic staples. The hope, of course, is that you'll drop something into your cart.

Both ends of the aisles feature specials of the week. Called end caps, some are good deals, others aren't; but you have no way of knowing since you can't compare the $3.29 bag of Tostitos's tortilla chips to other brands. They're back on aisle 4.

Whether we know it or not, the supermarket world is a carefully orchestrated shopping experience, and we are unwitting participants. "Supermarket designers know your heart," wrote Jack Hitt in the *New York Times Magazine*. "Their layout is a chaotic opera of flattery, soothing you with a wealth of options, making you feel that you're a chef picking over the finest meat, the most delicate in fresh greens, the best in imported condiments, even as your cart fills with familiar hamburger meat and iceberg lettuce, prepared cake mixes, and maybe that new frozen popcorn shrimp you've heard about."[1]

In a typical shopping excursion, you will encounter more than 35,000 products, all vying for your shopping dollar.[2] To be on guard against making unplanned purchases, make sure you have a "tight" grocery list after going through your refrigerator and pantry.

It helps to know your prices so that you're not shopping by instinct. Begin by studying the weekly supermarket flyer that you received in the mail or picked up at the front of the store. What's on sale this week? Whole chickens? Russet potatoes? Greek yogurts? If they're great deals, then adjust your shopping list and go with the price breaks; you can have sloppy joes the following week when hamburger goes on sale.

The supermarket flyers also feature the store's "loss leaders" for the week—foods, goods, or merchandise sold at cost or less than cost. These specials are designed to pull you into the store so that you'll do the *rest* of your week's shopping during the same trip. Supermarket executives know how much we enjoy the convenience of one-stop shopping.

If you really want to save some money, build your shopping list around the loss leaders at your regular supermarket as well as the competition. You might drop by Safeway on your way to the post office and Albertsons after soccer practice if they have specials on certain meats or products that are winners in your home.

Once you're in the store, take your time. You don't want to make buying decisions as fast as you can wheel your cart, grabbing familiar products and pausing occasionally for a quick label scan or price comparison. Instead, slow down. Don't rush yourself. Remember that you're *earning* money every time you make the right choice. Watch out for impulse purchases, which supermarkets love.

Historically, grocery stores earn a slim profit margin on staples such as milk, bread, sugar, and coffee. Where they make their money is in nonfood items like hair spray, lipstick, and deodorant and the prepared foods found at delis. With their tantalizing displays of fresh ground beef, thinly sliced mesquite turkey breast, delectable shrimp, and colorful salads, delis account for only 5 percent of a store's sales but 15 percent of the profits.

Another profit center is cereal, which is arranged by brand rather than by type (again, to make it tougher to compare prices). It's no mistake that sweetened cereals like Froot Loops, Corn Pops, and Frosted Flakes are at knee level, right where your small children can grab a box. If you need a demonstration that TV advertising works, there it is.

It's all about branding sometimes.

Battle of the Brands

When members of the Association of National Advertisers gathered at a convention one time, many were worried about a clear-cut trend: sales of store-label goods were continuing to eat into the market share of brand names such as Pillsbury, Pepperidge Farm, Ivory Soap, Folgers, Heinz, and Procter & Gamble.

More and more cost-conscious shoppers are snapping up house brand or private label products in recent years—with name brands taking it in the shorts. Private labels account for more than a 20 percent share of all grocery and consumer-product sales.

What's happening is that consumers have reached the limit on the price increases they can afford to shell out for essentially the same brand and package. In other words, why should you buy Advil when the Kirkland private label at Costco is exactly the same thing? Read the label: each tablet contains ibuprofen USP 200 mg.

Supermarket chains, in an effort to fend off stiff competition from the warehouse clubs, heavily promote their store brands. Many place their house labels right next to the name-brand products and hang stickers on the shelves that proclaim, "Compare to the National Brand and Save!"

That's a smart move by grocers. Store brands are anywhere from 20 to 50 percent cheaper than their name-brand cousins. What's even better for the supermarkets is that their profit margins are often higher than on their name brands.

Where do these private-label goods come from? Thanks to technological advances, lab scientists can break down the ingredients in about any product. Head and Shoulders shampoo? Chemists can whip up batches of dandruff shampoo in the same distinctive blue tint in no time. The result is a house-brand dandruff shampoo in a familiar white bottle with a wavy blue line for half the price.

That's why you see knock-off versions of Tylenol, Mylanta, Oil of Olay, Metamucil, Crest, and Pepto-Bismol—plus thousands of other products—for discount retailers.

Sometimes in the area of food, supermarkets purchase inventory from smaller manufacturers or from the brand-name producers selling off excess production. For instance, it's more cost effective for a Tree Top processing plant to keep a second shift running at full capacity by selling its surplus apple juice and applesauce to Kroger.

But what about quality and taste? When *Consumer Reports* conducted a taste test between name brands and store labels, they judged the differences to be nil. The magazine's conclusion for many products was, "No brand stood out. Shop by price."

Actually, I disagree. I've found considerable differences in quality and taste, especially for items like orange juice, chocolate chips, canned meats, ice cream, and canned vegetables. Some people joke that store-brand green beans are made up of end pieces. Häagen-Dazs ice cream certainly beats Safeway's Lucerne Neapolitan, and Hollywood mayonnaise tastes better than the cheaper stuff.

If you're okay with the variations in taste, I recommend buying store brands for the sake of economy. Sure, the store-label corn might contain a lesser grade, but you really have to be fussy to turn up your nose at smaller kernels of corn. If you're still not convinced, look at the price comparisons. Can you justify paying 20 to 40 percent more for minimal taste or quality differences? Of course, there will also be a few exceptions for personal taste, but when it comes to spending smart, reach for the store brand or private label.

Shopping Wisely

Here are some other ideas when you step inside a gleaming supermarket, ready to fill your cart:

1. Know your prices. Sometimes you should type out a list of grocery staples and comparison shop the supermarkets you like to frequent. Have a good attitude: it can be fun once you get going. You should compare the prices of your favorite cereals, ketchup, peanut butter, jam, ground beef, milk, bread, toilet tissue, paper towels, cough syrup, and so on at two or three supermarkets, plus a warehouse club (if you have one nearby).

My comparison shopping tests have shown that if I spent $135 at our local "bag your own groceries" chain, the same groceries cost $150 at our upscale neighborhood supermarket, around an 11 percent difference. That translates to around $1,500 annually for a family of four.

What about warehouse clubs for groceries? While

warehouse clubs have their limitations, you can save big bucks on groceries—around 33 to 48 percent. I'll talk more about warehouse clubs in the next chapter.

2. Take along your coupon stash. How deeply you want to get into coupons is your decision, but it's easy to find coupons for your favorite cereal, baby diapers, and personal care products. Also, look for the point-of-purchase coupons. Some have blinking lights to catch your attention. But be careful! That name brand *with* a coupon may not be cheaper than the store brand.

3. When meat goes on sale, don't tarry. With so many meals built around meat, you have to jump on meat sales. My favorite is when boneless chicken breasts drop from $3.99 a pound to $1.99 a pound, which happens like clockwork every month or so. We buy a dozen or two packages for the freezer and use the chicken for everything from stir fry to chicken parmesan.

4. Ask the meat manager when reduced meats—beef, chicken, and pork—are set out for quick sale. Most meat departments put their markdowns out at 9:00 a.m. on certain days of the week. Ask the same question of dairy and produce managers. If you cook a piece of meat that was marked down and it doesn't smell right, simply take the sticker back for a refund. (Most supermarkets will take your word, but because there are dishonest people in the world, some stores will want the meat back.)

5. Don't be afraid to ask for a discount in the produce section. Slightly bruised fruit and wilting vegetables can be heavily discounted because they are probably a day away from being thrown out, but you have to ask someone in the produce department. Believe me, supermarkets want it off the floor. Just ask, "What kind of discount could you give me if I purchase this bruised fruit?"

6. Ask for rain checks. This is my favorite loss leader: When single-serving Brown Cow chocolate yogurt, which normally cost 99 cents, goes down to two for a dollar, I'll grab the last ten chocolate yogurts from the shelf. Then at the cash register, I ask for a rain check, which means I can come back at another time and purchase more chocolate yogurt for half price!

7. Look for the "multi-buy" discounts. Many supermarket chains are discounting staples like milk by offering a package deal. If you buy two gallons, then the cost is $7, instead of $4 for one gallon. Go for it.

8. You can shop for food at swap meets. You can usually find two or three booths selling stuffing, boxed cereal, and canned food at swap meets. Be sure to check the expiration dates and inspect the packages for damage.

9. If you're a soda drinker, stock up on soft drinks during the big sales. Coke, Pepsi, and 7UP go on sale at least three times a year: Memorial Day, Fourth of July, and Labor Day. Soda stores well, and it can occupy a corner of your basement or garage for up to a year without losing quality.

10. Supermarkets offer huge savings the week before Thanksgiving. Stock up on items that don't go on sale during Christmas—jellied cranberry sauce, marshmallows, stuffing, sweet potatoes, and frozen turkey—if you're going to repeat Thanksgiving dinner at Christmastime. Remember, leftover turkey is great for making turkey sandwiches.

11. Shop the "scratch and dent" collection. Ask the store manager where they keep dented cans and damaged packaged goods. Who cares if the tomato sauce can is pushed in a little?

12. Stay away from costly prepared foods. Rotisserie chicken, coleslaw, potato salad, macaroni salad, frozen pizza, frozen dinners, pot pies, New York cheesecake, and goodies from the bakery department cost a premium.

13. Consider purchasing an old refrigerator or chest freezer to take advantage of big sales on meats, vegetables, produce, and drinks. But filling a fridge or freezer can be a double-edged sword. Fresh food rots after a week or two, and freezer burn hits after three or four months. Also, some older freezers and refrigerators slurp up electricity.

We have an old refrigerator in the garage to stash our bargains, but because of freezer burn, we'll have an "empty the fridge" week every few months.

14. Check out the day-old bread store. Most cities have places where you can buy day-old or just-about-to-expire bread products at considerable savings.

15. Shop natural health markets. They go by names like

Whole Foods, Trader Joe's, and Sprouts. They used to be really expensive, and Whole Foods—nicknamed "Whole Paycheck"—isn't cheap. But natural health markets have become much more mainstream in the last five years as health-conscious shoppers flock through their doors. If you shop wisely, you can find good deals on much healthier food.

16. If you prefer health foods, join a local co-op. The best way to find out about health food co-ops is to network with friends, check out craigslist postings, or read through the advertisements in your local newspaper.

17. Check to see if you have a "share" co-op program where you live. In some cities, you can buy several boxes of food for a nominal price. You don't have any say about what gets put into your box of foodstuffs, and you may be asked to perform several hours of community or volunteer service to buy these groceries at a significant discount.

18. Be careful if you have the munchies. Those who shop when hungry are more likely to buy impulse items—Christmas eggnog, taco-flavored Doritos, Dove bars, and specialty meats. Careful shoppers eat something *before* they shop.

19. Finally, take your time! Pushing a cart while juggling coupons and newspaper inserts, making price comparisons, looking for store brands, and wondering if a "sale" item is a bargain involves an investment in time.

Remember, each time you make a good decision, you put

fifty cents or a dollar into your wallet. When you're a smart grocery shopper, you're actually *earning* money.

And you can stretch your grocery dollar even more at warehouse clubs.

5

Get Thee to a Warehouse Club

At the end of tennis star Michael Chang's career, I collaborated with him in writing his autobiography, *Holding Serve*. For those with just a passing interest in tennis, Michael became the youngest male to win a grand slam tournament when he captured the 1989 French Open at the age of seventeen.

The unlikely victory for the Chinese-American tennis prodigy made him famous overnight and led to a successful tennis career that reaped more than $18 million in prize money and tens of millions more in endorsements and appearance income. Michael may be worth millions and way out of my financial league, but he's a man after my own heart. Let me explain.

One evening I was interviewing Michael over the phone. While I sat in front of my computer and tapped away, Michael answered my questions from his parents' home near Mission Viejo, a Southern California suburb. In the midst of our interview, Michael stopped to ask a random question.

"What time does Costco close?"

I glanced at my watch; it was just after 8:30 in the evening.

"Our Costco closes at 8:30," I said.

"I think the one near my parents' home closes at nine o'clock," Michael said.

"Why do you ask?" I queried.

"Because I have to buy some tennis balls."

"You mean you buy your tennis balls at Costco?" I immediately had this mental image of Michael Chang pushing an oversized cart topped off with ten boxes of Penn tennis balls through a cavernous, stack-it-to-the-ceiling warehouse club with shiny cement floors. I started laughing. The thought of Michael Chang buying tennis balls at Costco was like Rachael Ray dropping twenty-five-pound bags of flour into her shopping basket or NASCAR driver Jeff Gordon purchasing a set of four radials off the rack.

"Yes, I buy my own tennis balls at Costco," the tennis champ said. "I have to admit that I get a lot of funny looks at the checkout. Usually I get asked why I'm buying so many balls when I could get them for free from the manufacturers, but it doesn't work like that in tennis. We're not sponsored. I have to buy tennis balls just like anyone else."

I guess Michael likes saving a few bucks like anyone else, because buying his tennis balls at Costco—or buying anything in bulk—results in significant savings. I'm probably not telling you anything you don't already know, but in this chapter, I want to explain *why* warehouse clubs are cheaper nine times out of ten for their unique product mix of groceries, appliances, clothes, automotive items, and whatever happens to be in inventory that day.

But you have to keep your head straight when you walk into a warehouse club; otherwise, you might drop a $1,999 Sony flat-panel television into your cart when you originally ran into Costco to pick up some milk, bread, and a box of printing paper.

You can call it a blind spot, but I love warehouse clubs. I get a kick dropping a four-pound box of Grape-Nuts into my cart and knowing it's 40 percent less than the same amount at a supermarket.

As the old saying goes—a dangerous one, I might add— "The more you buy, the more you save."

Looking into the Background

My fondness for warehouse clubs dates back to 1976 when the first membership warehouse opened in my hometown of San Diego. An entrepreneur, Sol Price, leased an ark-like building on Morena Boulevard and began selling merchandise and business products at rock-bottom prices. Within a year, San Diego was abuzz: the Price Club had the most incredible prices in town.

Ah, but not just *anybody* could shop there. You needed to purchase a $25 annual membership card (plus $10 for family members). And to get one, you had to be a business owner or executive with a California sales tax permit, or be an employee of a bank, school, hospital, local utility, or city government—stable elements of the economy. The Price Club deemed these people as unlikely to shoplift or write bad checks.

Membership cards, which included the member's name and photo, instilled a feeling of "ownership" among the members and also fostered repeat trips. "If I paid $25, then I have to get my money's worth!" was the common cry. Membership fees also discouraged frivolous shoppers.

The strategy worked. The Price Club was an instant success. Talk at cocktail parties in nearby upper-class La Jolla centered around how to score a Price Club card. Membership, in this case, had its privileges: opportunities to buy remarkably well-chosen merchandise at low prices.

As the Price Club expanded and opened new stores, other companies jumped into the warehouse game: Sam's Club, PACE, Price Savers, Costco, and BJ's Wholesale Club. The industry zoomed during the eighties and nineties, but as "category killer" stores with price-competitive merchandise and more shopping options (I'm talking about stores like Office Depot, Toys"R"Us, Best Buy, Petco, and Men's Wearhouse), there was consolidation and mergers. Basically, a generation later, we have three major players in the warehouse club game:

- Costco, which bought out Price Club, is the largest membership warehouse club in the United States and

is the second largest retailer, behind Walmart
- Sam's Club, which is owned by Walmart
- BJ's Wholesale Club, which is mainly concentrated along the Eastern Seaboard

These days membership is not so restricted. Basically, if you can fog a mirror and pay the membership fee, you're in. Warehouse clubs provide entrée to a limited selection of quality national brands and private label merchandise with a wide range of product categories. Rapid turnover, high sales volume, and reduced operating costs enable warehouse clubs to operate at lower profit margins than discount chains and supermarkets.

Now, I know some of you may be thinking: isn't walking into a warehouse club a recipe for getting into *more* debt? Good point, but if you shop wisely and don't overbuy, you can save a couple of thousand dollars each year on high-quality merchandise and grocery items. So, whether you are a warehouse club veteran or wondering if you should make the plunge, here are some points to keep in mind:

Warehouse clubs have to make sense for you. If you live in rural Nebraska and the closest Sam's Club is four hours away in Lincoln, you shouldn't be jumping into your family Suburban when you run low on milk and eggs. If you're empty-nesters or just a household of two, buying forty-eight rolls of toilet paper, six pounds of breakfast sausage, and a two-gallon pack of milk doesn't make much sense, especially if you don't have an appetite to eat Jimmy Dean sausage for two weeks straight or enough room to store a mountain of toilet paper under your bed.

In their defense, warehouse clubs have gotten *much* smarter selling in smaller bulk sizes. It used to be that if you wanted to buy tomato sauce, you had to purchase a two-gallon can—marked "Restaurant Serving"—and somehow freeze the rest. Now warehouse clubs will shrink-wrap six smaller cans (each in a sixteen-ounce size) together for a single purchase. If you're making spaghetti sauce from scratch, then you only have to open one can.

The problem with warehouse clubs is that many are not conveniently located. Warehouse clubs are usually situated on the outskirts of suburbia where land is cheaper, or the only one in the city happens to be at the *other* end of town. If you are fortunate to live within reasonable driving distance of a warehouse club, however, then you're halfway home.

As mentioned before, there are only three players in the warehouse club universe: Sam's Club, Costco, and BJ's Wholesale Club. I have never visited a BJ's, because I've lived in California and Colorado all my life. I've belonged to both Sam's Club and Costco, and if given a choice, my pick is Costco. In my opinion, they have better products than Sam's, their return policies are the best in the business (if anything goes wrong or you don't like it, you can return it and get your money back), and they have the best free food samples.

Know your products, know your prices. Warehouse clubs' philosophy of limited selection means they can't afford to stock losers. That means their buyers have to make the right call, and I'm amazed at how often they get it right.

You might find only one brand of salami at Costco, but the Carando Genoa salami from Italy is so good that it would make *mama mia* homesick for the old country. The fresh-squeezed orange juice from a local producer tastes like a delicious sample you'd find at a Florida orchard. The black leather jackets are sewn together from soft, high-quality hides. Even the fresh-cut flowers are beautiful.

On items like television sets, stereos, computers, laptops, and other electronic goods, warehouse clubs offer low-end, midrange, and bells-and-whistles versions.

Not everything is a better deal. You can't walk around blindly and start pulling items off the shelves willy-nilly at a warehouse club. If you know your prices, then you're aware that the boneless chicken breasts for $3.19 per pound at Costco can usually be found for $1.99 per pound at local supermarkets once a month, which means it's a loss leader. Soda pop like Coke and Pepsi is usually cheaper at supermarkets for some reason. But nine times out of ten, as I said before, you're not going to go wrong buying soft drinks at the warehouse club.

Don't look down your nose at private label items. Costco

started the private label revolution by selling its own club brand called Kirkland, and I've been pleasantly surprised over the years: Kirkland stuff is good! From dried fruit to laundry detergent, I've found the quality to be very high. I'm even starting to see clothing lines, such as socks and shorts that are fashionable—and cheap.

When done right, private labels can offer tremendous savings. The warehouse clubs like them because private brands cut out the middlemen with all their brokering and advertising costs, but it does make it tougher to comparison shop when the item is not available elsewhere. I haven't found that objection to be much of a problem, however.

Secret Boss

To help you understand why warehouse clubs offer consistent savings on everything from soup to nuts and from tires to small appliances, I'm going to introduce Rich.

Rich and I have known each other for years, and he's worked in the warehouse club industry since the 1970s, when he started with Price Club in San Diego. He rose in the ranks and has been the manager at several different Costco stores. Rich agreed to answer my questions about the warehouse club industry as long as I agreed not to disclose his identity.

Q: What's the average markup on merchandise?

Rich: The general markup is 8 to 8.5 percent. From that

amount, we deduct payroll (4 percent), benefits (1.5 percent), utilities and supplies (.5 percent), taxes (1 percent), and central overhead and real estate (1 percent). All those expenses add up to 8 percent. Here's one of our bigger secrets: without membership fees, Costco would not be profitable.

Q: You mean you don't make any money on the merchandise?

Rich: That's right. If it weren't for the annual membership fees, we couldn't stay in business. It can be honestly said that we sell merchandise at cost, and our profit comes from membership fees, which approach 2 percent of sales. That's not much room for error in this business.

Q: It used to be that warehouse clubs were good places to buy toilet paper and paper towels but not groceries. Now you can buy just about any food item you want. What happened?

Rich: Over the years, we had a change in business philosophy. Grocery items increase the *frequency* of shopping. Everyone has to eat, and milk lasts only one week. Food appeals to everybody.

Q: What are your bestselling items?

Rich: It's still toilet paper and paper towels, but eggs, milk, meats, and frozen items are always top sellers.

Q: What are supermarkets doing to compete?

Rich: Supermarkets have tried to stem the growth of warehouse clubs, but they cannot move the merchandise as efficiently as we can, nor can they generate the volume necessary to support low prices. The "club buster" sales are actually loss leaders for the supermarkets. Their newspaper ads may feature these items, but they hope you don't buy them.

Remember: the average markup on supermarket items is between 22 and 28 percent. Our limited selection increases efficiency. You won't find twenty-two different brands of peanut butter or forty different kinds of cookies at a warehouse club. But we have to make each item on the floor count. We operate by the "Six Rights of Merchandising." Simply put, that means we have to have the *right merchandise* at the *right time* in the *right place* in the *right quantity* in the *right condition* at the *right price*.

The right merchandise includes new and exciting products. We have to sell what the members want, which generally means name brands, but we're starting to see buyers flock to our private labels.

Q: What do you mean by that?

Rich: At Costco we started the private-label revolution by selling our own club brand called Kirkland. Since then private-label goods have grown significantly in market share. That's why you see supermarkets pushing their own store brands. Some commodities such as laundry detergent and soda pop are easily "knocked off," and smart shoppers recognize there isn't much difference in quality.

Q: Is that why it's difficult to comparison shop electronic equipment, such as TVs and Blu-ray players, because the model numbers never match up?

Rich: Exactly. A lot of name-brand manufacturers create special versions for warehouse clubs—and electronic stores like Best Buy—with different model numbers or face plates. How can a customer compare a Costco Sony Bravia TV, which may have an extra feature on it, against a Sony over at Walmart?

One way to get around this barrier is to do an Internet search, but that takes time and energy.

Q: I've noticed that warehouse clubs carry high-quality merchandise and name brands but have a limited selection. What's the reasoning behind that?

Rich: Limited selection increases efficiency. With fewer vendors to order from and fewer items to stock, fewer mistakes are made. Errors cost money. It is also easier to maintain a limited selection. Can you imagine what life is like for the "reorder" specialist at Home Depot? "Let's see, we have 1,001 bolts, 1,002. . ."

In fact, I think limited selection is the primary strength of warehouse clubs. Let's say you walk into a Best Buy with their walls of televisions all playing the same Disney video. Where do you begin to shop? How do you know one television is better than another? I'd rather let the warehouse club buyer make the decision for me than the sharkskin-suited salesman feeding off commission. That's why we offer excellent products in three price ranges: low-end, midrange, and high-end.

Limited selection makes shopping easier and clearer for the customer, because we often bring in items recommended by *Consumer Reports* magazine, although we can't advertise that fact. But we know our customers tend to read such publications.

By focusing on limited selection, the Costco purchasing agents gain economies of scale all along the distribution pipeline. "Another truckload of televisions for Costco? Yup, you weigh the same as the two trucks ahead of you. No need for a full inspection. Just roll on through."

Believe me, those little savings count. Another part of the magic is transporting full loads because freight rates are much lower in full-truck quantities as compared to less-than-a-truckload shipments.

Q: Sometimes I'll see some really off-the-wall goods, like Gucci handbags and Swatch watches. Where do warehouse clubs get those?

Rich: We sometimes purchase goods "unconventionally" on the gray market. For example, Levi Strauss may not want to sell to a warehouse club because that would upset The Gap or Banana Republic. But then one of those traditional retailers will approach us with an overstocked item, or someone in the distribution chain will divert those goods to us. We have to authenticate the merchandise, of course, because there are counterfeits out there! If we sold fake Seiko watches, for instance, we would lose a tremendous amount of goodwill.

Sometimes buying unconventionally involves cloak-and-dagger maneuvers. Once, a local tire store was selling Michelins for less than our wholesale prices. We sent a truck over—unmarked—and bought as many tires as we could. When our truck left, their manager tailed our truck to see where it was going. Our people knew they were being followed and made sure they lost him before delivering the tires to our distribution center. It really gets wild out there.

Q: What shopping tips can you give our readers?

Rich: Get to know some of the staff. They can tell about the hot bargains or when something new is expected to arrive. They'll know which slow movers have been marked down or when prices changes are made. For instance, Costco usually changes prices on Saturday nights after closing.

Take a close look at the numbers on the listed price. At Costco we identify items on initial breakdowns by a price ending in 97 cents. These have been marked down from the regular priced items, which end in 99 cents.

Odd pricing, such as items that end at 89 cents, 79 cents, or 49 cents, indicate that these are specially priced items that Costco got a deal on from the manufacturer. These can be better deals than at other stores, but it's usually not better than the 97 cents prices.

When you see an asterisk on the upper right side of the sign, that means the item won't be reordered. Anything that ends in 88 cents or .00 cents is a manager markdown. Sometimes managers will slap that price to move a product very fast.

There's also a little date in the lower right-hand corner, below the price, that indicates the last time the price was changed. This doesn't mean the price is lower now, but there was a price change of some type.

So there you have it, folks, a little peek into the world of warehouse clubs. If a warehouse club is within a reasonable distance from your home, buy in bulk as much as you can. Then shop at the supermarkets once a week for fresh vegetables and items you can't purchase at a warehouse club. Doing so will give you the best of both shopping worlds.

6

Let's Go Out for a Bite to Eat

The summer I turned sixteen, I had a huge appetite that had trouble keeping up with an adolescent body growing by leaps and bounds. I ate seconds and thirds so often that my mother wondered if she should peel up some kitchen linoleum and serve it fried.

That summer one of my mother's cousins, Bob Hoffmann, rented a room from us because he was taking some college courses nearby. We called him "Uncle Bopper" because of his crazy sense of humor. One evening as he watched me wolf down my third pork chop and second baked potato, he announced a brilliant idea. "You know that HomeTown Buffet in Pacific Beach? I think Mike and some of his friends could eat that place out. They'd run out of food if we had fifteen hungry eaters like Mike. Then I could sue them for breach of contract and false advertising."

Uncle Bopper was kidding, of course, but he liked the idea of sending a swarm of hungry adolescent males into an unsuspecting buffet to see what would happen. So we enlisted some heavy eaters in the neighborhood, about a dozen in all, and even made up team T-shirts. On a Saturday night, our troupe walked into a HomeTown Buffet type of restaurant. We hadn't eaten in *hours*, so we were starving. As we giggled and punched each other in the shoulder, Uncle Bopper asked to speak to the manager.

"You see these kids?" he began. "They are poised to consume all the food you have. We can settle this right now, or I can turn these voracious eaters loose." Then Uncle Bopper whipped out a parchment containing a lot of Latin legalese and subjunctive clauses. The legal-looking but bogus document set forth the demands to settle the threatened "lawsuit."

It was all a put-on, but the manager was a Greek immigrant who didn't quite comprehend what was going on. Managerial training school had never prepared him for this sort of challenge. "What does this mean?" he asked, pointing to the parchment.

"It says if these kids eat everything you have, then you have to pay treble damages for false advertising and breach of contract, since this is an *all-you-can-eat* establishment."

The baffled manager shrugged his shoulders. He muttered something in Greek and then replied, "Be my guest."

My friends and I attacked the buffet line, filling our plates with salads and breads. Then we returned and devastated the fried chicken and roast beef entrées. It was a mismatch—like the Notre Dame football team against a high school squad. The kitchen scrambled to keep up, but when we returned for seconds on roast beef, the slices were decidedly rare and cool to the touch.

After watching us gorge for an hour and a half, the manager asked to speak with Uncle Bopper. "Please, sir, can you tell your boys to stop? I've only been manager for one month."

We were stuffed anyway, so Uncle Bopper called off the dogs.

That evening at the country buffet was probably the last time a restaurant lost money on me. These days I still count eating out as one of life's joys, although meals out these days are getting really expensive. But it's nice to be served, eat a delicious meal, and have somebody else do the cleanup.

When eating out, it's important to pay attention to *value*. Sure, you and your family could chow down at Joe's Greasy Spoon for ten bucks a head, but oily food and dirty forks make for an unpleasant dining experience that will still set a family of four back $50, when you add in tax, tip, and drinks for the kids.

At the other end of the spectrum, you and your family could dress in your Sunday best for an evening at L'Hermitage, where you could indulge in a gustatory delight of *gigot d'agneau aux flageolets* or *escalope de veau aux morilles*. But that would cost you a car payment—something north of $300.

Sensible restaurant eating falls somewhere in the middle. But before I get into some smart spending strategies, let's take an overview of the industry.

From Diners to Fine Dining

The least expensive eateries are *coffee shops*, *diners*, and *cafés*, where the clientele often look like they've stepped out of a ZZ Top video and the waitresses wear beehive hairdos. The menu—mostly short-order fare—can range from inedible to tasty, but the price is right: $5 to $7 for a hot breakfast of eggs, bacon, and toast to $8 to $10 for hamburger and fries to $12 for chicken fried steak and mashed potatoes. And it's fun to people-watch in diners.

The emphasis is different at *fast-food restaurants*, where high volume and quick turnaround are gospel. An assembly-line process produces burgers, hot dogs, tacos, burritos, sandwiches, and fries in a hurry. Families with young kids frequently eat in fast food restaurants, especially when they are on the road. Although "dollar items" have disappeared in recent years—another sign of the times—you can generally fill a tummy for under seven bucks and small kids for half that.

The next step up is *"fast casual" chains* like Panera Bread and Chipotle Mexican Grill, which emphasize the quality and freshness of their food, as compared to the processed foods—canned or frozen—often served in fast-food places and budget restaurants. Traffic at fast casual restaurants have outpaced their counterparts in recent years as consumers find that healthier food, reasonable prices, quick service, and clean, sit-down surroundings hit their sweet spot.

Costing the same but struggling a bit are *moderately priced restaurants* such as Denny's, Village Inn, International House of Pancakes, Shoney's, and Big Boy. The service is good and you don't have to dress up. The waitresses cater to families with high chairs for infants and crayons for kids. The menu focuses on breakfast fare, burgers, sandwiches, salads, and "skillet" meals. I also include ethnic restaurants in this category: Italian, Mexican, Chinese, Thai, Indian, Japanese, and German. Many are family owned and serve delicious meals, albeit spicier, at moderate prices.

The next level up encompasses *sit-down restaurants*, where a hostess or maître d' escorts you to your table. Chains like Olive Garden, Red Lobster, and Mimi's Café have carved out a niche in this space, although high-end Italian, Chinese, and Mexican restaurants can also be found in this category.

The ultimate experience is *fine dining*, the bastion of Food Network fans and lovers of haute cuisine. White linen tablecloths and napkins grace your table, lemon wedges flavor your water, and a lighted candle and a fresh rose add a touch of class. The lighting is muted, and live piano music fills in the background.

A well-trained waitstaff attends to your every need. The menu is stripped down, and portions are small. The chef puts as much emphasis on how the food *looks* as on how it tastes; presentation is everything. You order à la carte, so you can expect to pay a separate price for an appetizer, salad, entrée, dessert, and coffee. If you drink wine, that's a costly "upsell" as well.

No matter where you eat, from the humble blue-collar breakfast joint to the fancy restaurant with valet parking, it's going to cost you more than you think. At sit-down restaurants, it's difficult to enjoy lunch for under $10 (for one person). When you add in sales tax, tip, and a beverage; that number is closer to $20 at dinnertime. At the hoity-toity places, you can figure on spending at least $50 if you include a salad and dessert.

Granted, restaurants are a labor-intensive industry struggling to make a profit just like any other business. But these days it can cost a family of four a cool $75 for a ho-hum hamburger, fries, and lemonade meal on a Tuesday night, which is a lot of money for a no-frills meal. And many times at the more popular restaurants these days, you're rushed to "turn over" the table after an hour.

So how do you keep a lid on restaurant spending? Here are some ideas to keep in mind.

Make eating out an "occasion." Perhaps you've experienced this scenario in your house: Dad arrives home from work just as Mom pulls into the driveway with the kids after soccer practice. It's 6:00, and everyone is tired and hungry. Dinner hasn't been started yet.

The next thing you know, your family is sitting down at a nearby Italian place. The kids' spaghetti is bland, and you're not impressed with the chicken cacciatore. But the $65 tab catches your attention.

Eating out should be reserved for an *occasion*. It doesn't have to be a special one like for a birthday, graduation, or anniversary, but impromptu meals should be discouraged. If you eat out on a Thursday night, what's your family going to do on Saturday night when it would be nice to do something special by going out to dinner together? Restaurant meals should be planned for and anticipated.

If the above scenario happens in your home, you might want to consider these alternatives:

- Cook something fast, like grilled cheese sandwiches and a healthy soup you keep stocked in the pantry.
- Better yet, eat up your leftovers. Dad and the kids can pitch in and help Mom.
- Pick up something ready-made—like a pizza—at your local supermarket. If the idea is to get something hot into your tummies, pizza always works. It's not exactly the healthiest choice, but at least you don't have to tip the delivery person.

If you and the family decide to go to a sit-down restaurant anyway, you can trim your bill by taking advantage of early bird specials, using two-for-one coupons that come in the mail, or ordering the "special" of the evening, which is often a three-course meal. Weeknights are great nights for specials, and some restaurants let kids eat free to bring in more traffic.

Don't worry what the help might think of your discount dining. Restaurant owners and managers do not resent customers who use coupons—or shouldn't—because customers add to their cash flow. The main reason the waitstaff is wary is because they fear a smaller tip. You should tip the usual 15 percent on what the full amount would have been.

Order complete meals. Look for entrées on the menu that come with appetizer, soup, or salad. In restaurants where salad is à la carte, order the bigger salad and share with your spouse or family member. When scanning the menu, remember that chicken is always cheaper than fish, fish is usually cheaper than beef, and beef is always cheaper than lobster.

Do "date nights" during lunchtime. When times are tight, one of the first "spending cuts" couples make is going out. Consider doing your "date nights" during the lunch hour, when entrées are a third less than on the dinnertime carte. If your kids are in school, you'll also save on paying a babysitter.

Drink water. Not only is water healthier than soft drinks, but ordering soft drinks can soak up gobs of money.

Watch the add-ons. The waitstaff is trained to get you to order appetizers, the more expensive specials of the day, and dessert. If you indulge in each area, you can easily double the cost of your meal—and take in enough calories to keep you on the treadmill for a week.

Go out for breakfast. Scrambled eggs, an omelet, or oatmeal are quite reasonable.

Purchase a "dining club" membership. Nearly every major city has a dining club that offers two-for-one entrées. Restaurants in different price ranges and food styles participate. The annual membership is between $25 and $50.

If you're traveling to an out-of-town soccer game, pack a lunch to eat along the way. Where is it written that a family must worship at the altar of McDonald's anytime it drives an hour from home? A cooler filled with sandwiches, rice cakes, chips, trail mixes, string cheese, fruit, and granola bars should make the kids happy.

Double-check the check. All too often, errors are made, and for some reason, they usually aren't in your favor. If you think you've been overcharged, ask humbly if a mistake has been made. If you've been *undercharged*, point out the mistake, because it's the right thing to do. More often than not, the mistake in your favor will be waved off and your conscience will be clean.

Be leery of group checks. Have you ever eaten with a bunch of friends—somewhere between six and twelve—and then wondered what to order because you're not sure how the bill will be split? *Hmmm, should I get something expensive? Because if everyone else is ordering big, I don't want to order something cheap and then be stuck paying a lot more.* It can be a little frustrating to eat spaghetti *carbonara* for $15.95 while everyone else is ordering New York strips for $27 and then hear your share of the bill is $35.

Dining with a large group can be a delicate situation, especially if the check is placed in the hands of someone at the far end of the table. We all know waitresses don't like doing separate checks. Most of the time, you're going to have to shrug off any inequality or go ahead and order a more-expensive entrée like everyone else. It isn't easy taking charge in a group atmosphere.

Although it's out of character for me, I do remember the time I acted assertively. I was eating with a group of fifteen, and I ordered a vegetarian entrée for $10.95. But several guys at the end of the big table went hog-wild, having the waitress bring out plate after plate of appetizers, lobster thermidor, and chocolate lava cake for dessert. The wine flowed freely, too, but I didn't imbibe.

When the check arrived, they informed me that my share was $32 with the tip. "Hey, I ordered the vegetable lasagna, drank water, and didn't have any appetizers," I interjected. "Here's $15, which should more than cover my share of the bill with tax and tip." It was hard for them to argue with the truth.

If you're dying to go out, make it dessert. A lot of upscale steak houses are known for their molten chocolate cake that flows like a lava explosion or their foot-high slice of mud pie. If you're looking to have some fun on a budget, dropping in after dinner for a yummy dessert can be the sweet exclamation point to the day.

If you're traveling long distances, get off the main drag. A restaurant tucked away on a side street, away from the pricier real estate along Main Street, should be a better deal. Those places often are family owned and have a lot of character.

Along the South Carolina coast a couple of years ago, we followed the back streets to a sandwich shop backing up to a coastal inlet. No one told us that a crocodile was going to be swimming off the back porch!

Adding It Up

Do you know how much you and the family are spending in restaurants each month? On drive-thru trips to McDonald's and Taco Bell? If you're inputting your receipts into Quicken, then it would be a good idea to take a peek. If you're not tracking your eating-out expenses, however, then I can take a good guess for you. According to the National Restaurant Association, the average American eats food prepared in a commercial setting one out of every five meals, or 4.2 meals per week.

For a family of four, that means eating out seventeen times a week. If you figure that you spend an average of $10 per meal (I'm trying to balance the difference between fast-food meals and sit-down restaurants), that's $175 a week, or $700 a month.

I wonder if my estimation of $10 per meal is too low, because it always costs more to eat out than you think. Let's say you invite the family to TGI Fridays, one of the better chain restaurants that seem to be all over the country. You and the two children go easy, passing on the Sesame Jack Chicken Strips appetizer ($12.59) and the Jack Daniel's Salmon and Shrimp Scampi ($22.49), which looks too pricey. Instead, you and your spouse settle for two Blackened Chicken Alfredo meals at $15.29, which is more than you wanted to spend, but you justify the expense because the entrees come with house salads. As for the two growing kids, they're happy with cheeseburger meals for $8.79 each. Mentally, you're figuring around $50, plus tip.

But then you order two iced teas for the adults and sodas for the kids—bottomless drinks for $2.49 each. Although your waitress does her best to entice you with the dessert tray, you stand firm and order only one Brownie Obsession ($6.49) and four forks so everyone can share. Finally, you round off your evening with two coffees at $2.79 each.

So, what's this Fridays meal on a Wednesday evening going to cost you? When you add 8 percent sales tax and a 15 percent tip, the amount comes in at $86.34. But many folks think that eating at Fridays is cheap! Well, Fridays is cheap when you compare it to a tablecloth-and-candle type of restaurant, where the entrees start at $19.95 and zoom up to $37.95. The fact remains that it cost more than nearly $90 for the whole family to eat out at a fairly ordinary place in just one hour!

Okay, so you blew your budget by going to TGI Fridays on a Wednesday evening. On Friday night, you're tired and don't feel like cooking, so everyone piles into the minivan for a trip to Mickey D's—McDonald's. It's a lot cheaper to eat there, but it was still $20 for Premium Crispy Chicken Bacon Clubhouse sandwiches, fries, and Happy Meals for the kids.

Finally, on Sunday after church, your best friends invite you to join them at Winnie's Diner, a family-style restaurant that's big on Formica tables and has waitresses who call you "honey." Winnie's is cheaper than TGI Fridays, but not by much. In this instance, "Sunday supper" costs $70 out the door. So, looking back at the week, you and your family ate twelve restaurant-type meals—less than the national average—but you still spent $175, which, if you did this every week over a month's time, would come out to $700.

That's too much money, especially if you're trying to get out of debt. Listen, I'm no fuddy-duddy; I love to eat out as much as the next person. I look forward to the time of unhurried conversation, the period of family interaction, and the respite from the daily routine. The problem I have is that we pay dearly for the convenience, especially in restaurants that charge $80 for bland "mesquite" chicken breasts, nothing-special hamburgers, soggy fries, flat Cokes, and overpriced chocolately desserts in a deafening atmosphere.

If more families spaced out their trips to various restaurants, then significant savings could be realized. If those midweek forays to Fridays, Chili's, and Applebee's are killing you, eating at home a couple of more times each week will save you an easy $350 per month.

The National Restaurant Association says that we spend 47 percent of our food dollars in restaurants, compared to 25 percent back in 1955.[1] Since one out of every five meals is eaten in a restaurant-like setting, that means we're spending 48 percent of our food dollars on 20 percent of our meals. There's an imbalance here, and a place where some fat can be trimmed from our expenditures.

Cooking at home more often is a great way to spend your food dollars a lot more wisely. In the next chapter, I'll describe some ways to make cooking in your kitchen easier for you and healthier for your family.

7

Love That Home Cookin'

The answer to eating out less is dining in more.

Anytime you cook at home, you're spending your money wisely. And I mean *cooking*, not popping a frozen dinner into the microwave. Anytime you can do the chopping, dicing, carving, crushing, peeling, sawing, snipping, and splitting, you can pocket the labor savings—and also create delicious meals.

My fear is we have lost the ability to chop and dice, to bake and broil. Not only is our culture losing the ability to cook, but we are losing the desire, and that saddens me. I can still remember Andrea and Patrick returning from a sleepover and telling us what they were served for dinner—macaroni and cheese from a box, warmed-up pizza left over from the night before, or even cold cereal.

I think there is a tremendous benefit—besides the financial aspect—to eating a hearty home-cooked meal with everyone around the table. The communal can-you-pass-the-corn talk prompts bigger discussions in which the family can talk about their day and about their hopes and dreams in the safety of those who love them. You may think that I'm as old-fashioned as a Norman Rockwell painting on the cover of a

Saturday Evening Post magazine, but I believe that eating a "regular" dinner together is the best investment you can make in your family—financially *and* relationally.

Sure, it's difficult to get everyone together with soccer practices and Boy Scouts and Wednesday night youth group meetings to work around. We adjusted by having a dinner hour that flexed with the kids' schedules. We delayed many meals until 7:30 or 8:00 on weeknights so all of us could sit down and eat together. We survived waiting until the last child got home from a tennis match or school play practice.

Financially, let me make this point. If you look at eating at home as a money-saving measure, this means your kitchen becomes a profit center—a place where you're *making* money each time you make breakfast, lunch, and dinner.

It's amazing what you can save when you cook meals at home or do some of the manual labor to prepare your food. Take chicken, for instance. Cutting up a whole chicken takes two or three minutes, but that's a daunting task for many. All you need to do is watch a how-to YouTube video and have a sharp knife available. You can also buy bone-in chicken breasts and debone them and take the skin off.

Cooked shrimp is another example where DIY works. If the supermarket's meat department shells and deveins the little crustaceans, you pay $29.95 a pound. But if you buy cooked shrimp with the shell and veins, you could be paying $15 to $17, almost half the price. Convenience foods such as prepared salad, coleslaw, boxed rice or potatoes, frozen battered chicken, frozen vegetables in steamer pouches—they all cost considerably more. Can you cut the ends off fresh string beans before you steam them? Then buying them in the produce department is going to be considerable cheaper for you and your family than the canned or frozen versions.

Using your freezer to take advantage of meat sales is a good idea. If you see top sirloin for $4.48 a pound when it's usually double that, then by all means stock up on a meat that can be used for a variety of dishes—from fajitas to stroganoff to barbecue.

How long does frozen meat last? Butchers will tell you that if you rewrap the meat in freezer paper and tape, it should easily last three to six months before freezer burn sets in. Always remember that it's "first in, first out" when you take something out of the freezer.

Frozen fruits such as blueberries, blackberries, and strawberries are great to keep around for smoothies. One thing some shoppers aren't aware of is when fruits and vegetables are in season. These days supermarkets are importing more and more produce from Mexico, Central America, South America, and even New Zealand. An uninformed (or unconcerned) shopper may see New Zealand strawberries in January and Costa Rica avocados in July and plop them in the cart, but those items might cost two or three times more than in-season produce from US farms and orchards.

Since homegrown fruits and vegetables cost much less during the summer, consider blanching and freezing your favorite fruits and vegetables for the winter, especially if you have a backyard garden or like to shop farmers' markets. If you're looking to save money on canned and frozen vegetables, be aware that growers and wholesalers want to liquidate their inventory at the end of the summer. Early fall is a good time to stock your pantry for winter.

Once-a-Month Cooking

Back when I was editor of *Focus on the Family* magazine, we featured Mary Beth Lagerborg, a Denver mom, standing in her kitchen, peeling and chopping onions and carrots. Mary Beth and a close friend, Mimi Wilson, had recently published a book titled *Once-a-Month Cooking*, and it soon became a runaway bestseller.

Mary Beth's and Mimi's concept boiled down to this: do most of your monthly grocery shopping in one day, cook all of the next day, and store the ready-made meals in the freezer. It was an interesting formula and an idea that struck a chord with many busy moms. When I told my wife, Nicole, about this "once-a-month" concept, she immediately turned up her nose. "Why would I want to do that?" she asked. Nicole *loves* to cook.

But after the *Once-a-Month Cooking* book came out, I read the testimonials of those who said once-monthly cooking worked for them. My feeling was that if you want to make it work for you and your family, then go for it. The concept revolves around browning chopped onions and lots of hamburger meat and diced chicken breasts at one time—twenty to thirty pounds—and then packaging the cooked meats in one-pound freezer bags. When you need a meal, you pull a bag of cooked hamburger or sautéed chicken breasts out of the freezer, heat up the cooked meat quickly in the microwave or a pan, and voilà—you have the fixings to make tacos, chili, spaghetti sauce, meat-and-rice, or a casserole in a matter of minutes.

I couldn't get Nicole interested in getting behind the concept. She didn't want to have twenty bags of cooked meat in the refrigerator, ready to eat at a moment's notice; she likes some spontaneity to prepare and serve something she feels like eating that night. But instead of going for once-a-month cooking, Nicole found that *thrice-a-week* cooking worked well for us.

This meant when cooking, Nicole prepared enough of the main dish that we could get at least another meal out of it. When she did that three times a week, the family was basically covered if we threw in a restaurant meal. I heartily recommend thrice-a-week cooking. If that sounds like something that could work, then keep the following points in mind:

Leftovers taste great. Great-tasting meals are just as good when heated up one, two, or three days later. Having leftovers in the fridge is the perfect answer to those evenings when you're too tired to cook or haven't shopped or are running out of time. Some leftovers taste even better the second time around. For instance, mixing leftover spaghetti noodles and spaghetti sauce in a big pan with butter or coconut oil and heating it up is absolutely delicious. Coconut oil carries tremendous health benefits because it's high in omega-3 fatty acids.

Have a freezer stash. I think browning twenty pounds of hamburger meat and packaging the cooked meat in freezer bags is over the top, but it wouldn't hurt to have a couple pounds of cooked hamburger or diced-up chicken in the freezer for an "emergency" meal. A few tortillas, shredded cheese, and you can make chicken quesadillas in a jiffy.

Use your slow cooker. Every couple gets one as a wedding present. Don't let it gather dust. Fill it with browned meat, vegetables, chicken broth, and water in the morning, and you'll have a great meal that evening. For those moms who work outside the home and are too wiped out to cook at the end of the day, doing the food preparation before you leave the house—while the kids are getting ready for school—could be a great solution.

Buy a bread machine and a food processor. Bread machines are ridiculously cheap and so useful that every kitchen should have one. When you eat your own fresh bread, it's hard to go back to Wonder bread. As for food processors, these slice-and-dice machines can shorten thirty to forty-five minutes of food preparation time—time you don't have—into five minutes. Once you get the hang of using a food processor, you'll wonder how you ever went through life without one.

Pack a lunch to work. When I worked in an office, I have to admit to a twinge of jealousy when my coworkers got together and left to go out to eat while I stayed behind with my brown bag lunch. A peanut-butter-and-jelly sandwich, some chips, and an apple were waiting for me in the company refrigerator, but I was saving $8 to $10 a day, or an easy $200 a month. I told myself that I would rather spend that money on my family than on myself.

There was one other thing I noticed: it was hard for my coworkers to eat out in less than an hour. Sometimes lunch was a ninety-minute break, which meant they had to work thirty minutes longer than me. I started working at 7:30, which meant I was out the door at 4:30, having put in my eight hours. They were there until 5 or 5:30, depending on when they started work.

The same brown bag advice goes for the kids. A few bucks may not seem like much for a school cafeteria lunch, but multiply it by two or three kids and five days a week, and it adds up. You could even teach your children to make their own lunch, which gets them used to being around the kitchen, providing for themselves, and understanding that they don't have to be served every time they're hungry.

8

Never Pay Retail

I'll never forget the time I stood among the ladies' dresses at Foley's, an upscale department store in Colorado Springs. It was just before 8:00 p.m. on a Saturday evening, a few minutes before the next "dress riot."

What was a "dress riot"? I didn't know, but I had been told that it was a ten-minute clearance sale on specially marked clothes. A crowd of thirty shoppers—okay, they were mostly women and a couple of guys—were milling around, waiting for the shoe to drop on the next sale.

I was at Foley's for research purposes. During the countdown, I casually asked one of the salespeople why these events were called "dress riots."

"Oh, we don't like to use that term," she replied, "but that's what they really are. You should have seen the last dress riot this afternoon. Two women grabbed a $229 navy-and-white Pendleton ensemble at the same time, and then they began fighting over it because it was marked down to $19.99. You should have seen them rolling on the floor, trying to pull the dress from each other's grasp. Finally, our manager took a bullhorn and announced, 'Ladies, if you don't stop right now, I'll have to call security!'"

"Things really got that crazy?" I asked.

"They sure did."

Just then, four clerks wheeled out four dress racks, each containing fifty to seventy-five pieces. Bedlam broke out as a horde of women stormed the barricades to grab the heavily discounted dresses, all priced at $14.97.

A friend of mine, Karen Sagahon, reached for a white Leslie Fay dress with black polka dots, but a man brusquely swooped it off the rack—along with twenty other dresses. Karen shrugged her shoulders. "I guess I'm not a fighter," said the diminutive young woman, who weighed slightly over a hundred pounds.

The dress riot was over in five minutes. Poof! One hundred and fifty dresses vanished, except for an odd-colored straggler or two. The feeding frenzy left the clothes racks resembling goldfish carcasses stripped by a school of piranha.

Another friend, Lou Gage, managed to hold her own. She claimed a half dozen dresses, although she wasn't shopping for herself. Lou told me that she enjoys buying dresses and passing them on to friends. One ended up in my wife's closet: an azure-blue Liz Claiborne with white buttons, originally $148. We were glad to pay Lou fifteen bucks in reimbursement.

The dress riot was the highlight of Foley's "Moonlight Madness Sale," a sixteen-hour, shop-'til-you-drop bargain bonanza. Lou stayed until half past eleven, finding good buys in women's accessories and shoes. The next morning she laid out all the clothes and merchandise on her living room floor, added up the receipts, and compared them to the original retail amounts.

On this particular shopping excursion, Lou spent over $500, but the regular retail amount would have been $3,085, an 83 percent savings. "I've never done worse than 82 percent, and my best is 90 percent," she said. "It's gotten to be a challenge: *How much can I get off?*"

The Shopping Game

Granted, most of you aren't going to buy $500 worth of clothes at a clip with the idea of giving them away. And it's likely that you may not have "dress riots" at your favorite department store. But Lou's experiences are a reminder that those who seriously shop department store sales can purchase high-quality clothing at a fraction of the original price.

But department stores aren't the only shopping game in town, no siree. There's a zillion websites selling clothes, shoes, and accessories, and there's no doubt that online shopping— with the convenience of never leaving your home—is a huge draw for busy parents. There's also no doubt that high-end department stores like Neiman Marcus, Nordstrom, Saks Fifth Avenue, and Macy's are under intense pressure these days. The last ten to fifteen years have seen various retail store chains—Broadway, Carter Hawley Hale, and Joslins—enter

Chapter 11 bankruptcy or be picked up for pennies on the dollar by other companies.

In this chapter, however, I'm going to be talking about shopping at brick-and-mortar stores either close to home or in the big city near you. As I've noticed from watching my wife, Nicole, shopping for clothes is a personal experience. You have to touch the fabric. Try it on for fit and fashion. And compare the article of clothing to something else you like. That's why shopping for clothes online will always be at a disadvantage—you can't try the clothes or shoes on before you buy.

That said, shopping for clothes in person happens in these sorts of stores:

Perched at the high end are the aforementioned *department stores* like Neiman Marcus and Nordstrom that anchor sprawling malls. They often sell merchandise at a full markup, but in recent years there's always some sort of "sale" going on. High-end retailers pride themselves on customer service and shopping assistance. Best of all, they have liberal return policies.

The best buys are in quality clothing, luggage, silverware, jewelry (but not fine jewelry), and household items. While department stores are generally crowded, especially on weekends, if you play your cards right, department stores can be a great dollar-for-dollar deal. You should also look for "rack" outlets in major cities, which are stocked with unsold goods and returns from parent stores. Because of their liberal return policies, you might find twice-worn pumps for $29.95 instead of $149.95.

Power retailers like Walmart, Target, Sears, and JCPenney have the financial muscle to buy in huge quantities and push vendors for discounts, which can be passed along to consumers. Prices, especially at Walmart, can be very low.

The best buys are in children's and infants' clothes, baby furniture, ladies' clothing, accessories, and household items. Some have said that fashions at these stores are not cutting edge, but that is no longer true. Many times, though, sales lack variety and certain sizes because the stores are getting rid of end-of-season merchandise.

Next, we have *moderately priced stores* like Gap, Old Navy, Banana Republic, and Izod, which seem to be everywhere—downtown streets, suburban malls, and outlet stores. Styles are hipper, or seem that way, since so many people dress in clothes purchased from these brand-name stores. Blue jeans are big sellers as well as polo shirts and long-sleeved button-down shirts.

Stores such as Ross Dress for Less, Marshalls, and T.J. Maxx are called *off-pricers*. They buy from a variety of manufacturers and vendors—or buy closeouts from department stores—and work off a smaller markup. The selection may be limited and the styles a season behind. Few special services are offered. There's a "treasure search" aspect to shopping at Ross Dress for Less or T.J. Maxx, because once items are gone, they're gone. You can often find some great deals on unexpected items, like luggage.

Many of these stores don't have sales. Their selling philosophy is to add another 25 percent discount to their low-markup regular merchandise.

Warehouse retailers such as Costco and Sam's Club buy in huge quantities from manufacturers willing to cut them a good deal. Selection is limited, but with minimal markups, prices are excellent. Except for jackets, you can't try the clothes on in the store, but they're easily returnable. Some find this a hassle—some don't, especially those who enjoy a good bargain.

If you don't mind taking clothes home to try on and then bringing back those that don't fit right, then shopping at warehouse clubs can be a good change of pace.

Factory outlet stores have sprung up outside many major cities, often thirty to sixty minutes away by car. Manufacturers such as Nike and Eddie Bauer sell surplus production, returns, or discontinued merchandise. Outlet malls are good places to shop while you're on vacation, although you have to watch out since there's a tendency to loosen the purse strings too much while on holiday.

Playing the Game

Big discounts can be had at all these stores if you know how to play the shopping game. Nearly every retail store has a selling system that boils down to this: move the end-of-the-season merchandise when the next season of clothes arrives. Because stores have to make room for their hot-selling profit makers, no one should ever have to pay retail for clothes. Someone is always having a sale or just about to have one. Be patient.

You may think you can't afford a new dress for your daughter's eighth-grade graduation, but I say you just have to work at it. You start by getting familiar with the way clothing stores sell things. If you can invest a few hours, then you can find what you want at a price you can afford. You do this by buying clothes off-season or during the stores' big sales three or four times a year.

An example of buying off-season would be walking into Target a few weeks before Labor Day. The summer merchandise has got to go because the fall and holiday stuff is arriving. That means you should buy your children's shorts or short-sleeve shirts after Labor Day—not in the spring when they're sold at full retail. The same goes for other seasonal items, such as winter coats, gloves, and beach sandals. Although it may seem weird to buy a ski jacket in April, you'll be glad you did the following November.

Many people don't shop at department stores because the clothes are expensive. That's understandable when you're paying regular retail. But if you wait for their once-a-quarter sales, you can purchase high-quality merchandise at 50 percent off or more. Remember, quality clothes last longer and look better.

As for buying on sale, you do that by:

- shopping the department stores' "doorbuster" sales three or four times a year
- keeping an eye out for sales at the off-price stores, such as Ross Dress for Less and Marshalls. Many of them are not advertised.
- checking out the clearance racks
- looking for closeouts at the clearance stores
- knowing prices so that when a deal comes along, you can pounce on it

Huge department store chains sell clothes for dimes and nickels on the dollar to rid themselves of excess inventory headaches. Play your cards right, and you can find great prices on leather handbags, shower curtains, towels, small area rugs, children's shoes, sheets, bedspreads, and pillows—items hard to buy on a discount. The markdowns often average 50 percent.

Before attending a big department store sale, you should be adequately prepared.

Check out your expenditures for the month. Do you have enough set aside to do some clothes shopping?

Know what you want to buy. Does your husband need

some new dress shirts? Do your teenage son's blue jeans have holes? (Wait a minute. . .blue jeans with holes are more valuable!) Make a list so you can shop with focused goals.

Go the night before when the markdowns are being made. Typically, all the advertised markdowns are made between 6:00 p.m. and closing. If you find something you like, you can usually buy it at the next day's discounted price. All you have to do is ask.

Leave the kids at home. They'll get bored, and you'll get on each other's nerves. Plus, you need to concentrate on the task at hand.

Arrive five minutes before the store opens. Early birds really do get the best worms, especially at the doorbusters that run from eight to eleven in the morning. In blow-out sales, the size selection is often skimpy.

On the morning of the sale, the first thing you should do is ask for the ten-minute special sheet and the ad for the "doorbusters." You can usually find these online or at the information counter. If the salespeople say they don't make the sale sheets available to the public, ask to look at them. They generally will not refuse such a request. Be sure to take notes of the ten-minute specials' "batting order."

Scan the ten-minute special sheet and figure out which ones you can skip. You can use that time to run things out to the car, get a bite to eat, or visit the restroom.

Follow the ten-minute specials. These are the extra

markdowns made on clearance merchandise that has already been marked down several times. You have to be fast on your feet.

Don't carry a purse; use a fanny pack. You need freedom and flexibility as you hurry from one ten-minute special to the next.

Shop for classic styles. Buy jackets, slacks, skirts, shoes, belts, and purses to match basic color schemes. Don't buy fad items. Buy in one classic, tasteful color scheme so replacements are easy to find. You can always add an accessory to update the style or color.

Taking your husband along can be a two-edged sword. On the one hand, he can help stand in line at the cash register while you go on to the next special. Then again, he may get grumpy. (I'm speaking from personal experience.)

Keep your cool. Have a spending limit in mind and stick to it.

Shopping at Home

While websites selling clothes are doing a better and better job of making the experience more user-friendly and offering free shipping once you hit a certain price point, you sometimes have to pay return shipping when you want to send a clothing item back.

The same goes for those who shop from the comfort of their couch. QVC and the HSN (Home Shopping Network) own this space, selling billions of dollars' worth of goods each year. Despite the rise of online shopping, shopping while watching TV shows no sign of disappearing.

The shopping channels sell home furnishings, jewelry, electronics, clothes—just about anything. The prices are generally good. You might be able to buy clothes by fashion designer Diane von Fürstenberg for half of what a department store would charge. Many of the fashions sold on TV and online appeal to plus-size women who prefer to shop anonymously and not in a crowded mall.

You have to be careful stepping into the world of shopping channels. It can be like getting sucked into a vacuum cleaner. You're bored one afternoon or late one evening, flipping through channels, no Häagen-Dazs in the freezer, when you land on QVC or HSN. You see a gold-filled chain for sale, and while you never thought you needed a second or third gold chain, you like the look and the price, and the next thing you know, you're ordering.

You're among the millions of people who fall for these impulse buys every day. When you channel surf, steer clear of the merchandise being hawked on TV.

You'll spend money smartly that way.

9

Trash or Treasure?

I've been talking about buying new clothes, but what about purchasing *used* clothing?

Some people don't like to wear clothing that someone else has worn; I get that. But used clothing makes sense, especially outfits for infants, toddlers, and elementary school-age kids. Some of the more common sources of good used clothing are garage sales, estate sales, thrift shops, consignment stores, and hand-me-downs from friends and relatives. Let's take a closer look at these options.

Garage Sales

I grew up in a home that majored in garage sales. Every Saturday morning, my mother took my brother and me to a half dozen sales, and we always had a great time sifting through other people's gems and junk. When our kids were younger, we carried on the Saturday morning tradition. It was inexpensive family fun, and Andrea and Patrick loved the "treasure hunt" aspect. More importantly, they learned valuable lessons: the value of a buck, how to bargain, and humility. They learned that we shouldn't be too proud to wear or utilize someone else's used stuff if it's in great shape.

Garage sales make sense, especially for families with young children who leapfrog from one size to the next every fortnight. Garage sales can also be a great place to pick up used sports equipment, which is an unexpected budget breaker for families. Better yet, you don't pay sales tax.

Here are some ideas that may prove helpful in shopping garage sales:

If you have a special need, ask God to open the door. Because going to garage sales is like shopping for the proverbial needle in the haystack, we usually need a miracle to find those cute OshKosh B'Gosh overalls for the baby or used baseball mitts for the Little Leaguers. Praying with your children can build everyone's faith, especially when you find the items on your prayer list.

If you're on the lookout for a particular item, such as a high chair, don't be afraid to ask the people holding a garage sale if they have one for sale. They may not have bothered to put it out.

Be prepared by doing your homework. Finding out about garage sales is actually more difficult these days because people have stopped listing them in the classified section of local newspapers. Searches on craigslist or your local "patch" online newspaper are good places to start.

Bring plenty of cash, especially fives and ones, as well as a roll of quarters. Some garage sales, especially the bigger ones involving two or three families, often run out of change.

Start early. As you go through your newspaper's garage sale listings as well as any you netted from an online search, check off the promising ones. Do any start at 8:00 in the morning? If so, you want to hit those first so you can arrive on time for the 9:00 sales. (You can also be a little sneaky and arrive a little early for the 8:00 sales to get first dibs.)

A significant part of the shopping strategy is *when* to arrive at a garage sale. Sometimes when a start time of a sale is listed as 9:00, it really means 8:00. People do this knowing that if they advertise an 8:00 opening, dealers will show up on their doorstep at 7:00. Other families, however, say 9:00 and mean it.

Being an early-bird shopper can work for and against you. If you arrive early, you have first crack at the bargains. If the prices are right, you're a winner. If the prices are high, however, the sellers may not be in a mood to bargain because they're expecting more customers.

On the other hand, if you arrive late in the morning or in the early afternoon, you can pick up some great bargains on unsold items. The last thing the family wants to do is cart their junk back into the house. They want it out of there!

Go to garage sales in up-and-coming neighborhoods with young families. Neighborhoods with young families are more likely to have items you're looking for. These families tend to sell nice children's clothing, the latest toys, and classic books simply because their kids have outgrown them. And they often have lots of things to sell.

Every city features great, good, and mediocre neighborhoods for garage sales. The most affluent parts of town are not always the best sections to shop because wealthy people tend to be older. Their adult children have been gone for decades, so you won't find any toys or children's clothes. But you might find a nice dining room table or china hutch.

Be a good bargainer. Most sellers expect to be chiseled down. If you're buying several small items that add up to $5, offer four bucks. A buck saved is a buck earned.

Sometimes people don't do a good job displaying clothing. They may set out several cardboard boxes filled with children's shirts and pants, but after several people have rummaged through them, everything is a mess.

Don't be deterred. Look through each item carefully and imagine what the shirt or pants would look like after being washed and ironed. Are there any holes? Any buttons missing? Permanent stains?

Look for brand names: Gap, Banana Republic, Carter's, Guess, Diesel, L.L.Bean, Van Heusen, and Wrangler. Nike, Reebok, and Adidas are top brands for sneakers.

Shop garage sales during your children's preschool years. Until your child is at least six years old, you can do a lot of your shopping at garage sales because the clothes haven't faded and usually don't have holes. They're just outgrown.

Little girls' dresses are another good buy. Top-end dresses, which retail in stores for $30 to $100, can be found at garage sales for less than $10. You shouldn't pay more than a buck for used children's books and DVDs.

Make sure the item isn't torn or broken. Shopping garage sales requires serious consideration of the saying "*Caveat emptor*," which means "Let the buyer beware."

You can't trust anybody these days, even at garage sales. Always check out electrical appliances—irons, blenders, TVs, computers—by plugging them in and seeing how well they work. Remember, it won't be worth paying someone to repair an appliance.

You're on surer ground with furniture, among the most sought-after merchandise at garage sales. Tables and chairs are big sellers because they cost so much less than retail. Sellers have the upper hand here. Buyers will have to make a snap judgment on whether the price is fair and fits their available funds.

Be on the lookout for "moving sales." Families relocating to another city or state are typically more willing to bargain on chests of drawers and dressers. You know people are serious about getting rid of their stuff if the garage sale is held during the winter or in the chilly fall or spring months. Often, garage sales in cold weather are a sign the family is either desperate or about to move out of town. Not only can you bargain accordingly, but you won't be competing against many shoppers.

Estate Sales

Estate sales are a whole different breed from garage sales. By definition, estate sales occur after a death in the family. The surviving family members, or a third party, often sell off the effects. Thus, estate sales are more organized. Since they're often held in private homes, those holding the estate sale limit the number of buyers who can enter. They naturally want to prevent light-fingered customers from shoplifting Grandma's silverware and jewelry.

Unless you arrive before the advertised time (which will *not* be moved ahead), be prepared to stand in line with antique dealers who are on the prowl for new pickings.

Prices are generally nonnegotiable in the morning. If you want to negotiate, ask, "Are your prices firm?"

The person behind the table may reply, "We are firm until 1:00 this afternoon."

Your next question is: "Are you going to go to half price then?" If he or she says yes, come back at 12:30, make your selections, and hang on to the items until 1:00.

Thrift Stores

Thrift shops are found everywhere, but it's hard to generalize which one is better. In your town or city, St. Vincent de Paul may be better than Goodwill, or the Disabled American Veterans store may beat them all.

In most states, thrift shops do a fine job of reconditioning clothes by repairing holes, doing a thorough cleaning, and ironing the article before putting it out on the sales floor. If you're wondering whether your favorite thrift store reconditions clothes, smelling them will give you a good indication of whether they've been washed and cleaned.

Thrift stores offer great deals. Infant overalls, which wear like iron, may cost $25 new at Target, but they're $5 at a thrift shop. Likewise, with garage sales, you want to be on the lookout for quality name brands.

When college students and young couples are starting out, thrift stores provide inexpensive places to shop for forks, spoons, plates, towels, and all the little items needed to furnish an apartment. A new towel, for instance, may cost $15 or $20 in a department store but just a couple of dollars at a thrift store.

The best time to shop thrift stores is in April, May, and June after people have done their spring cleaning. Another good time is at the end of summer—and before college kids arrive in town. Families who hold garage sales during the summer often box up the stuff that didn't sell and donate it to their favorite thrift store.

If you need a bed and can't afford new, then try shopping for a used one at a thrift store. For those a tad queasy about sleeping on a used bed, thrift stores often wrap new "ticking" material around the mattress so that the fabric is essentially unused and reconditioned. You can also purchase bed frames at Goodwill.

The best thing about thrift shops? They're wonderful places to buy costumes for yourself or the kids, or for the church's annual Christmas pageant.

Consignment Stores

Like a Mercedes Benz dealer who sells "preowned" cars, consignment stores view themselves as a cut above thrift shops and secondhand stores. Many consignment stores are middlemen who sell name-brand clothes in superb shape. A good-sized city may have a dozen consignment stores, which can be found with an online search.

Consignment stores sell a broad spectrum of high-end merchandise. You can buy everything from an expensive dress to a full-length mink coat. You're going to pay more than garage sales prices, but you're also going to pay less than retail. Consignment stores with names like Rags Fifth Avenue or Second Hand Rose will sell you single-owner evening dresses, ladies' wool suits, expensive furs, fashionable blazers, and accessories like leather belts, hats, purses, and shoes, all at tremendous discounts.

How much of a discount? You can figure 50 to 80 percent off retail. In a retail store, a woman's Pendleton wool suit might run $200 for the jacket and $100 for the pants. At a consignment store, you can buy both pieces for $60 to $90, and the Pendleton suit will look like it hasn't been worn. If you're shopping for an Easter hat, that fashion accessory will be somewhere around $5 to $15, a considerable discount from $30 to $50.

Consignment stores offer a wide selection, with varying sizes, colors, designs, and styles. If you have a teenager going to the senior prom, these shops carry the latest fashions at prices you can afford. Consignment stores are always fun for browsers. Keep in mind, however, that some offer only children's clothes while others cater to adults.

In comparison to their distant thrift-shop cousins, consignment stores offer a pleasant atmosphere—well lit, nice décor, and a fresh smell. One stipulation is that all clothes coming into the store must be either dry cleaned or laundered before they can be set on the rack. Most consignment stores keep half of the sales price and pass the other half on to the previous owner.

If you're in the market for second-hand sports equipment, check out craigslist or stores like Play It Again Sports or Recycled Sports. Used gloves, cleats, skateboards, and surfboards can be great deals. You should also keep an eye out for seasonal "swaps" where bikes, skis, soccer shoes, and hockey equipment are sold on a Saturday morning at a church fellowship hall or community center. To find out when such swaps are held, network with parents who have children in a particular sport, or you can call someone like the league commissioner or coach. And be sure to check the bulletin boards where games are played.

Buying at the end of the season is another way to save money. Purchasing a snowboard in April is going to be cheaper than buying one between Thanksgiving and Christmas.

Friends and Relatives

Hand-me-downs from friends and family can be a great way to pare your clothing budget. I can still remember receiving boxes of kids' clothes from relatives at times when we badly needed them. Then when our kids outgrew them, we passed them on to other relatives.

Don't be bashful about making your needs known for hand-me-downs—and then watch the Lord provide. It's important to get the word out among your friends and relatives that you would gladly receive donations of clothing, boots, books, and toys, and send them back when you're done with them.

That's what I call going full circle.

10

Flying the Friendly Skies

I am not a professional traveler, and I do not pretend to know the ins and outs of a turbulent industry that sends nearly 100,000 flights into the air every day.

I will say this: it's not difficult to spend smart when it comes to booking air travel and hotel reservations, thanks to search engine websites like KAYAK.com or Google Flights or any number of travel-related sites like Expedia, Orbitz, Hipmunk, Travelocity, and Booking.com. Another website that I like a lot—TripAdvisor—contains a huge bank of user reviews that give you the lowdown on the resort or hotel you want to book. You sometimes have to wade through a lot of mixed reviews, but you will get honest feedback.

I've found it's better to book directly on the airline's website. Generally speaking, the best place and cheapest price to buy a United ticket, for example, is from United.com. Ditto for the other legacy airlines as well as the low-cost carriers like Southwest and Allegiant Air. The best part about booking directly with the airline is that when something goes wrong, you don't get sent back to Expedia or Travelocity; you deal directly with the airline.

Today we don't see "airfare wars" like we did years ago—due to mergers and fewer airlines on certain routes—but there are some things you can do to tip the scales more in your favor:

1. Plan ahead. No, make that plan *way* ahead. If you're going to see family—especially during a holiday time—the sweet spot to buy tickets is between two and three months out—and six months if you're traveling during a major holiday like Thanksgiving or Christmas. Of course, purchasing tickets way in advance is a two-edged sword since airlines have nonrefundable ticket policies.

But if you know the kids get out of school on Friday, December 18, and you're planning to fly to your parents' home in Florida on Saturday, December 19, there's really no reason to wait. And if you're using frequent flier miles, then you really have to book in advance—like 330 days, which is the first day you can book on most airlines.

2. If there is a fare war, be ready to pounce. Historically, fare wars strike several times of the year. March and April are the months when summer sales are held. What the airlines are saying is this: "If you'll tie up your money with us for three to six months, we'll let you book your summer holiday."

Discounts are advertised just before and after Labor Day for travel up until Christmas, and just after the New Year, you can find winter and spring fares good until Memorial Day weekend. Don't expect dynamite deals to Orlando in the month of February, however.

3. Buy your tickets on Tuesday or Wednesday. Airlines know that most people do their online shopping on weekends, when they have more time. Consequently, the airlines tweak their prices a tad higher on the weekends and drop them back down in the middle of the week.

When airlines raise and lower prices, they are practicing "seat management," in which computers set the prices based on anticipated demand. That's why it's good to check different routing or flying through a different hub city with a different airline. If sales are slow for a particular flight, the computer stimulates sales by lowering the rates.

4. Find out when "off-peak" times are. Flights that are convenient for business travelers—who pay the freight for the airlines—are early morning and late afternoon. Naturally, the computers are going to keep the fares on those flights higher. But traveling before 7:00 a.m., late morning, early afternoon, or after 8:00 p.m. can result in significant savings.

Then there are "peak" and "off-peak" *days*. Don't expect to get the deal of the century on Thanksgiving Eve. You might be able to fly cheap at 7:00 a.m. on Thanksgiving morning, however, and still make it in time for turkey dinner. Or perhaps you return on Saturday instead of the Sunday after Thanksgiving. If you fly a little off-kilter, you can get a good price.

5. Be willing to fly red-eyes. This may be a daunting

prospect, especially with kids, but if a middle-of-the-night flight saves the family several hundred dollars, you're being paid well for an evening of sleep deprivation. Maybe you'll get lucky and the kids will sleep.

6. Consider driving to a different airport. When we lived in Colorado Springs, I found that our family could often save significantly if we drove sixty miles north to DIA—Denver International Airport—instead of flying from the Colorado Springs airport.

Of course, it has to be worth your time to drive out of your way to another airport. But if a couple of hours can save the family several hundred dollars on a cross-country fare, make the drive. The expense of driving and parking, however, has to be weighed against the savings you realize.

7. Volunteer to get bumped. When you check in for a busy flight, tell the agent your family is willing to be "bumped" to make room for late-arriving passengers. The airline will usually put you on the next available flight and compensate you with vouchers for future travel. Nicole and I have volunteered to be bumped several times, and the going rate is around $200 to $250 each in flight vouchers. If it's the last flight of the day, you can often get a hotel voucher, too.

8. Complain when flights go wrong. When an airline messes up—canceling a flight, sitting on the tarmac for three hours, leaving you stranded overnight in some faraway hub—send an email. Patiently but forthrightly describe what happened and ask if there is anything the airline can do to rectify the situation.

My complaints—all legitimate—have netted me discount vouchers good for future flights or a frequent flier bonus. The airlines want to keep you happy because they know unhappy passengers tell all their friends about their bad experience. But in the last few years, I've heard there is more pushback from airlines that are basically saying to customers, "Tough luck."

9. When going on vacation, stay with family and friends. Family is family, so it saves a lot of money when they open their homes to us and vice versa. When we've been invited to stay with family or friends, we've tried to be the best guests ever—cooking meals, helping with the cleanup, taking out trash, and even mowing lawns. By staying out of motels and coffee shops, we have saved an easy $200 a day.

10. Rent a condominium. A one- or two-bedroom condo is comparably priced to a standard hotel room with two double beds, yet condos have full kitchen facilities. Cooking for yourself, or at least eating breakfast and snacking in your condo, can cut your vacation food bill by more than half.

11. Shop for meals at supermarkets. For breakfast, you can carry out yogurts, fruit, bagels, and donuts. Full-service supermarkets have great delis for lunch, and their fried chicken dinners are considerably less than KFC.

12. If you have to book a hotel, call the hotel directly and ask, "Can you quote me your best price?" or *"Do you have any promotional rates during my stay?"* Hotels are notorious for not quoting you the best price unless you ask for it. This is even true in comparison to online shopping.

13. Consider using Hotwire, Hotel Tonight, Priceline, and other online sites to book "opaque" or hidden hotel deals. You don't know where you're staying until you put in your credit card and make the purchase, but you save big money every time you need a hotel room. Travelocity's Top Secret Hotels and Expedia's Unpublished Rates operate off the same idea. They claim that you'll get at least 25 percent off the lowest online rate.

Hotels need to fill rooms, and one of the ways they do it is to quietly sell deeply discounted rooms through hidden-deal sites. Hotels aren't like airlines, meaning they can't cut back on capacity, so they're aggressively looking for ways to book rooms, especially for last-minute travelers.

I've used Hotwire with great success, even on the day I wanted to stay in a room. On a few occasions, though, I think I've been given the key to one of the "Hotwire rooms"— perhaps not as nice a room, but that's been the exception and not the rule. I usually book a Hotwire room a class or two above where I would normally stay and have found that works just fine.

Priceline's system is a little different in that you "bid" for rooms on a particular date, star rating, and area, but if your bid is not accepted, you can't bid for another twenty-four hours. But whatever booking engine you choose, there are some real deals to be had if you're okay with not knowing what hotel you're getting before you buy a nonrefundable night's stay.

14. For a different type of vacation, consider Christian family camps or conferences. A weeklong stay at a Christian family camp often appeals to both parents and children. Usually held in scenic retreat areas, these camps provide meals, plan family activities, and offer varied accommodations according to all tastes and budgets.

The Christian Camp and Conference Association (ccca. org) is the best place to go for information on Christian camping. The costs vary widely. If you're looking for a "dude ranch" experience with all the bells and whistles—horses, overnight pack trips, traveling cooks—you'll pay $1,000 a head for a week of sleeping in luxurious log cabins with down duvets. But many Christian camps offering simpler facilities— called "rustic" in the brochures—charge $100 to $200 a week for each family member. Many of these camp and conference ministries are subsidized by parent organizations, which is why they can offer more attractive prices for families. Some facilities offer scholarships for families in need.

15. Stay in "gateway" towns just outside national parks or major tourist attractions. Since the US Forest Service allows only a few concessions inside national park boundaries, you'll pay a premium for sleeping inside the park. If you can find adequate lodging twenty miles away, it may be half the price. Ask hotels or motels if they have a AAA discount, which is often overlooked. The savings can be more substantial than you think.

16. Choose hotels and motels that offer breakfast. More and more lodging establishments, like Holiday Inn and La Quinta, are setting out cereal, muffins, and Danish pastries in the morning. Okay, the breakfast isn't substantial in terms of omelets and eggs Benedict, but if you and your kids have a bowl of healthy cereal, a piece of toast, and an apple or banana, you'll have enough fuel to last until lunchtime.

Many hotels and motels do not charge extra for children under eighteen who stay in the same room with you. If you have two queen-sized beds but five family members, perhaps someone can sleep on a blow-up mattress and sleeping bag on the floor. It's worth the savings.

17. If you're hitting the road, fill up your ice chest with ice and throw in your favorite drinks. Drinking water and juice will keep your kids happy—for at least the first fifty miles. Have healthy snacks available: energy bars, nuts, and fruit. Eating sugary treats can spark a sugar rush and possibly behavioral issues.

18. Part of spending smart is being vacation smart. Families, especially those with young children, need to think through what would be the best vacation, given the age of their kids. Let's say you have a three-year-old son and an eleven-month-old daughter. You think how nice it would be to take the family to Disney World. But Orlando is a thousand miles away—two long days of driving. And you only have one week off from work.

The obvious conclusion is that this is not the year to visit Mickey and friends. The kids are just too young and won't appreciate—or remember—the wonders of Disney World. And they will likely make the drive miserable, too.

Instead, you might consider renting a vacation condo closer to home at a nearby lakeshore resort or beach area. When our kids were about that age, we rented a friend's condo in the California desert city of Palm Desert in a complex with a nice pool. We all had tons of fun jumping in and out of the water. Life was simplified. Wait until your kids are in grade school for a big Disney trip, which, unfortunately, has gone through the roof in recent years. A family of four easily pays $1,000 for a three-day ticket at Disneyland or Disney World these days. And it will cost you just as much to eat inside the park and take home Mickey Mouse hats and souvenirs!

11

Why Gambling Is a Bad Bet

You won't find gambling as a line item in any family budget.

It's an expenditure that most husbands would do anything to keep their wives from discovering. It's also an addictive form of behavior that will take you and your family to bankruptcy court faster than any other pastime.

Although gambling is an equal-opportunity vice, I would be willing to bet that many more men gamble the family's rent money than women. Seriously, gambling is an insidious attraction that causes grown men to take leave of their senses. What else explains someone's compulsion to throw hard-earned money on a felt table in the faint hope of winning back that wager and something more?

I can still remember the last time I gambled, although it happened years ago before I got married. I was living in Mammoth Lakes, California, an Eastern Sierra ski resort three hours south of the bright lights of Reno, Nevada. Back then Nevada was the only state with legalized casino gambling, and an overnight jaunt to the "Biggest Little City" was just the antidote to Mammoth cabin fever. Reno advertised itself as a friendly, down-to-earth place, the type of neighborly locale where, as one friend told me, they smile when they take your money.

I was fresh out of college, collecting a minimum-wage salary of $3.35 an hour working at the Mammoth Mountain Ski Resort. As someone who had played his share of penny poker in the dorms, I was ready to test my luck at Reno's blackjack tables, which took a $2 minimum bet in those days. I can still recall my racing heart and the tingling excitement I felt as I fumbled for some folding money. I was going to walk away a winner!

In probably three minutes, I lost five hands and ten bucks. And then the most wonderful light in my head flashed on: *You mean to tell me that I worked three hours just to play five hands of blackjack—and lost it all?* I sure did, and that was the last time I played blackjack. I schlepped away from the horseshoe-shaped green felt table that evening and never gambled again. I even stopped feeding the slot machines a stray quarter or two rumbling around in my pockets. What was the point of working hard to fritter my money away so quickly?

With the passage of years, I can't believe how providential that was to learn my lesson about gambling so early in life— and for so little money. I'm reminded how fortunate I am each time I drop by a convenience store on a Wednesday night, where I witness a long line of folks waiting patiently to buy lottery tickets.

I actually feel sorry for them. Many of these people are working-class wage earners, friends and neighbors who hope against hope that their winning numbers will be the entrée to untold riches. I wish I could walk up to each one and remind them that the odds of winning are so low—estimated to be fourteen million to one and considerably worse if a "Powerball" jackpot is in play. They have a greater chance of being struck by lightning.

Just once, I would like to gather them with fourteen million others in a huge plaza so they could see how minuscule their chances are of winning a state-sponsored lottery jackpot. Finally, I would like to tell them that they are being played for suckers. Ten percent of all lottery players account for half of all lottery sales.

That makes me angry, because the last statistic tells me the people who can least afford it are betting the most on their futures. (Have you noticed that rich people don't play the lottery?) There's a term to describe those who play the lottery and visit casinos and bet on sporting events: *losers*, and they're usually in hock up to their eyeballs.

Across the Fruited Plain

Everywhere I look, state-sponsored gambling has become as American as apple pie. My home state of California, like forty-three other states and the District of Columbia, has had a lottery since the 1980s. State governments across the fruited plain pitch Lotto and Powerball like it's our civic duty to reach for our wallets and play their games of chance.

Looking at the Sucker Index, Georgia residents have been the most responsive: Peach State residents spent an average of $470 for every man, woman, and child![1] That's 1 percent of their annual income on a per capita basis. Can you imagine what your family of four could do with an extra $2,000 each year?

Let's be direct: Georgia and forty-seven other state governments (Utah and Hawaii are the only states that have outlawed lotteries or any form of gambling) are in the gambling business just as much as any Las Vegas casino owner, and they're trying to entice more gambling through the airwaves. "Everyone benefits from the lottery," claims a television spot in Virginia. An Illinois commercial urged residents to dip into their savings to buy Powerball tickets. During the holiday season, lotto tickets are pitched as the perfect stocking stuffers.

What a scam! Only half of every lottery dollar is paid out in winnings; the other half goes to administration fees or straight into state government coffers. If by some incredible chance you do win a decent-sized prize or a huge Powerball jackpot, the state *and* federal governments tax your windfall, taking 33 to 52 percent of your winnings right off the top! Furthermore, jackpots are usually paid out in twenty-year increments, so inflation makes each year's payment worth less than that of the year before. Once you deposit what's left, you'll be sure to hear from long-lost "friends" and relatives looking for a handout.

That's not what the public sees, however. They see a beaming truck driver with a John Deere hat holding an oversized check placard with tons of zeros while the media asks him how he's going to spend his newfound riches. Just once I would like to see the media interview lottery winners from past years and ask whether they are any happier now. I doubt they'd say yes. They probably spent everything they won on cars, houses, and lousy investments, but now they are staring at huge debts because these big-ticket items need maintenance and upkeep and their investments didn't pan out. They probably had hassles with extended family members who expected largess as well. When it comes to playing the lottery, be careful what you wish for.

I have a better idea for those who insist on playing the lottery. I would rather see them take a lighted match to several one-dollar bills on a cold day. At least they can warm their hands before watching their money go up in smoke.

Tentacles Reaching Everywhere

Gambling has exploded way beyond lottery and scratch-off games in the last ten years. Casino gambling has expanded into many more states, floating gaming parlors are back on the Mississippi River, and sports betting is common. I read a special report in *Sports Illustrated* a couple of years ago about the "dirty little secret" on college campuses—rampant betting on football and basketball games that generates much of the energy you see in arenas and stadiums. Bookies are everywhere, and many of them are students.

Gambling has become so big that Americans visit casinos more often than they attend professional sporting events. Collectively, gamblers lose more than $60 billion, which unfortunately is just a statistic and doesn't even begin to describe the human cost.

Dr. James Dobson, the founder of Focus on the Family who served nineteen months on the National Gambling Impact Study Commission, said he received too many disheartening letters from families whose lives were shattered by gambling. One was from Bob and Robin Cook of Lakeside, Montana, who sent their middle son, Rann—a good kid who went to church and was an honor student— off to college with high hopes for the future.

Away from home for the first time, Rann discovered video keno machines, the type of quick-play game that can suck money out of pockets like an air hose attached to a cashier's cage. (Video keno and video poker are so addictive that they are known as the "crack cocaine" of gaming.) It didn't take long for young Rann to lose everything he owned. He pawned his possessions, forged checks on his parents' checking account, and stole family belongings to feed his gambling habit. To protect themselves *and* Rann, Bob and Robin made the gut-wrenching decision to turn in their son to authorities. I can't even begin to contemplate the heartbreak that Bob and Robin felt when their son was incarcerated in state prison.

You don't hear stories like Rann's often enough. Families are often ashamed at the behavior of prodigal sons and husbands who gamble—and lose—feel as though they are leading double lives. My pastor told me one time that I would be surprised at the number of people in our church who've come to him for counseling regarding gambling debts. Those who gamble develop a propensity for betting money they can't afford on games they cannot win. It drives them crazy, and I can see why. You can never catch up.

Please, don't allow any sort of gambling to have a hold on your life. There are fifteen million compulsive gamblers in this country who wake up each morning wondering how they can make their next bet. I imagine that many don't want to live that way, but they're hooked by the adrenaline rush that gambling gives them.

You may think you have things under control—spending just a few dollars a week on Lotto tickets—but gambling is so addictive that you should adopt a zero-tolerance policy toward it. You're not going to get out of debt buying lottery tickets or playing craps or betting that your favorite pro football team is going to cover the spread on Sunday afternoon. You're going to lose your money and go into *more* debt.

You can, however, turn things around. Suck in a deep breath and realize that you need to take at least tiny steps each month toward paying down your debts. Not only will you be headed in the right direction, but you'll also experience deep self-satisfaction knowing that you're making headway through constant, consistent effort.

A Spiritual Perspective

After Roman soldiers nailed Jesus to a cross, "the soldiers threw dice to divide up his clothes among themselves," says Matthew. "Then they sat around and watched him as he hung there" (27:35–36 TLB).

Timothy L. O'Brien, author of *Bad Bet: The Inside Story of the Glamour, Glitz, and Danger of America's Gambling Industry*, says that story from Matthew enshrines "exactly who holds the high and low ground in the perennial debates about the morality of gambling."[2] Jesus obviously took the high ground as He paid the penalty for our sins on Calvary.

So is gambling a sin? Or just stupid?

You won't find any "Thou shalt nots" in the Bible regarding roulette or scratch-off games. Although the Bible does not speak directly to the subject, gambling does violate several major principles in Scripture:

• Gambling encourages greed (Luke 12:15;

1 Timothy 6:10; Hebrews 13:5).
• Gambling encourages materialism and discontent (Psalm 62:10; 1 Timothy 6:9).
• Gambling discourages honest labor (Proverbs 13:11; 28:19).
• Gambling encourages "get rich quick" thinking (Proverbs 28:20).
• Gambling encourages the reckless investment of God-given resources (Matthew 25:14–30).

The biblical principle of respecting honest labor and productive work disallows gambling. Seeking to get rich in a way that avoids respectable work violates scriptural truth.

Moreover, you're practically guaranteed that you will lose your money. A few years ago, everyone got excited when a Powerball jackpot reached $295 million, although it was reported that the odds of winning had risen to the stratospheric eighty-million-to-one range. That didn't stop a twenty-eight-year-old Bronx waiter named Ernie Kovic from going to the bank and emptying his $3,000 saving account—the one with all the money he had saved up for trade school tuition—to play one $295 million Powerball game. Sure, Ernie had three thousand chances to win, but he ended up being just one of the other 79,999,999 losers.

Maybe you think that the lottery is a sucker's play. Maybe

you think you can improve your odds by playing casino games: slots, roulette, craps, or blackjack. Sooner or later, however, the house will accept your hard-earned money—sometimes with a Reno smile and sometimes without.

So please, do yourself a favor and stay away from gambling. God will honor your obedience, and you can sleep better at night knowing that you are spending your money on things with a worthier return—such as providing for your family and paying off your stubborn debts.

New and Dangerous Territory

Being online means that you don't have to leave the comfort of your home to gamble.

At one time, you had to get to Atlantic City, New Jersey, or the state of Nevada to find a casino. That's no longer the case. Casinos are everywhere.

Online gambling is one of the most popular things to do on the Internet. All you need to do is a quick search and you can play popular casino games such as video slots, poker, and keno. Many sites allow browsers to gamble with "free" money to get you hooked. For those who like poker, you can play Texas Hold 'Em or Seven Card Stud against other players online, with the website taking a slice for staging the tournament poker game.

Internet gambling is generally considered illegal, but that hasn't stopped dozens of sites—many based offshore in the

Caribbean—from offering instant access to gambling. Have you noticed all the "pop-up" banner ads and full-screen links to casino sites whenever you're surfing the Internet these days?

Is Gambling Clouding Your Judgment? Three Questions to Ask Yourself

Have I fallen prey to marketing schemes? The fact is, casinos use all sorts of slick schemes to entice gamblers to risk as much money as possible. They often offer inexpensive or even free alcohol, which encourages drunkenness and thereby a decreased ability to make wise decisions. Everything in a casino is perfectly rigged for taking money in large sums and giving nothing in return, except for fleeting and empty pleasures.[3]

Am I becoming desensitized? The Bible tells us that we become what we think about (see Matthew 6:22–23). So if the focus of our minds is "getting rich quick" and we think gambling is the ticket, what are we becoming? Answer: desensitized to sin, pure and simple. Just because it's legal doesn't make it exempt from what God commands.

Am I trying to hide this part of my life? There are two types of people in the world: those whose problems are visible to everyone around them and those who attempt to carry around secrets. Sadly, way too many Christians try to live in the second category, which ultimately puts them in the first category—usually at a cost: broken trust, ruined credibility, labels like *hypocrite*. Don't let a secret come back to bite you. Make a change now. Come clean if you fear you have a gambling problem. Find a trusted Christian friend and confess your struggles.

12

Insurance for Assurance

Because Murphy's Law has stalked me all my life—*what can go wrong will go wrong*—I buy insurance on my car, my house, and my life.

I'm not going to talk about auto or house insurance in this chapter; I figure you're in "good hands," as they say. Life insurance is another matter because it's a long-term decision and a vital part of providing for your family if you were suddenly not here tomorrow. As James 4:13–14 (NLT) says, "Look here, you who say, 'Today or tomorrow we are going to a certain town and will stay there a year. We will do business there and make a profit.' How do you know what your life will be like tomorrow? Your life is like the morning fog—it's here a little while, then it's gone."

That reminder from Scripture is the reason why I buy life insurance, and the kind I purchase is term life insurance.

Term insurance, in case you're not familiar with the definition, is a voluntary arrangement between you and the insurance company based on whether you'll be alive at year's end. If you're still alive, the insurance company pockets the premium you paid. If you die, your beneficiary (usually your spouse) receives a rather sizable lump-sum payment to use to start rebuilding her life and provide for the children.

If you are a young father and were to die suddenly, the last thing you'd want to happen upon your untimely death is to leave your surviving spouse and children with a mountain of debt. The mortgage must still be paid, and credit card companies do not forgive your indebtedness just because you happen to pass away or die under tragic circumstances—such as terminal cancer or an auto accident.

Now, it's not my desire to be sexist in any way, but let's be realistic: term life insurance is mainly a guy thing. Since the husband is bringing home the bulk of the household income in most intact, two-parent homes, it makes financial sense to insure *his* life. The truth is that if he dies, the wife will probably prefer raising the children and not having to work full-time outside the home.

If the wife dies first, the surviving husband often keeps his job and makes child-care arrangements, such as having grandparents help out or leaving the children with a neighborhood mom who does daycare. I could be wrong here, but experience has shown this to be true. (If you are a single parent, then by all means I implore you to purchase term life insurance so that your children can be cared for in the event of your death.)

Term life is clean, simple, and easy to understand in comparison to the complicated and more expensive annuity insurance products like whole life, universal life, and variable life insurance, which are options. I understand that annuity or "variable" insurance products work for some people. If you've studied how they work and feel led to follow that investment strategy, I'm not here to squash your decision. As for me, I prefer to "rent" my life insurance by going with term life.

At one time, though, I had a whole life insurance product when the kids were young. For a mere $42 a month ("You'll never miss it," promised the agent), I received $30,000 of life insurance on myself and $20,000 on my wife, Nicole. Part of my premiums were placed into an interest-bearing, "cash-value" account that I could tap into at a later date, perhaps when the kids entered college.

For six years, my paycheck was clipped for $21 every two weeks for a total of $504 annually. That entire time I've never completely understood what whole life, universal life, variable life, or permanent insurance products were all about, but I figured they had to be good for my family because I had at least *some* form of life insurance.

The light came on when a middle-aged insurance agent attending the same church as me asked whether he could prepare a prospectus that plotted my insurance needs. I told him that I already had a whole life insurance plan, but he said that he thought he could present something better suited for my "growing" family. Since I was under no obligation, why not take a look at what he could come up with for me? I agreed to sit down with him.

When the agent handed me the prospectus, he said, "Your present insurance is not adequate. The insurance plan I'm offering will provide for your family in case you're no longer here."

You mean when I'm dead, I thought. I turned my attention back to the prospectus, which was really a pitch for a new whole life insurance policy. My head swam from all the figures and projections and expected payouts, but there was one figure I understood: the cost to insure myself with this "new" insurance product would increase my monthly premium from $21 to $300 a month, or close to $3,600 a year. I forget how much the death benefit was (now there's a funny phrase), but I think it was around $150,000.

I didn't have anywhere near an extra three hundred bucks a month to work with, so I declined, but that afternoon, I actually understood what whole life, variable life, or any other "piece of the rock" insurance was all about: my premiums were really an investment account with the insurance company, for which I received a death benefit and a return on my investment. When I studied the numbers in the folder, I was being guaranteed 4.5 percent on my money—as long as I paid in for seven years. If I opted out of the program before seven years, the "surrender value" would be negligible. (That's when I learned that the insurance agent's commission eats up most of the premiums in the first seven years.)

I reviewed my life insurance situation and decided that I had been traveling down the wrong insurance road. I became a believer in term insurance, especially after I did the math.

When I informed my whole life insurance company of my decision to drop out of the program, I had paid in $3,024 in monthly premiums over six years. I learned that my "surrender value" amounted to $1,800.

Bottom line: I paid $1,224 or $204 a year for two dinky life insurance policies that would pay for a modest funeral, a good wake, and six months of household expenses. I could have purchased a $250,000 term-life insurance product for $200 a year—much cheaper. I was in my midthirties at the time.

I will be honest with you: it was hard to pull the plug on that whole life insurance plan. No one likes to admit he or she made a bad choice on such an important purchase, and it wasn't easy taking a big gulp and placing that cancellation phone call to the whole life insurance company. A friendly voice attempted to talk me out of my decision, but I held firm because I knew I was paying very much for very little life insurance and receiving a pittance for the "investment" part of my monthly deduction.

If you're wondering what direction to go, ask yourself: *What exactly am I receiving for my money?*

Make a New Plan, Stan

Since then, I've been one of those "buy term life insurance and invest the rest" type of guys. Simply stated, term life insurance is the most cost-efficient way to provide for your family in the event of your death. It's easy to shop for—just type "term life insurance" into your search engine and you'll be presented with hundreds of options.

So, how much life insurance should you have? The recommended amount is eight times your annual income. If you are making $50,000 a year, then you should have $400,000 in life insurance. Here's another way to figure it: for every $1,000 a family needs to live each month, the widow should have $100,000 of life insurance. Using this equation, if your family has monthly expenses of $4,000 a month, then your wife will need a $400,000 lump-sum payment from the life insurance company. In this way, your surviving spouse could also receive some interest income if she were able to receive a 5 to 10 percent return on the $400,000 lump-sum payment.

No one knows better than I that even making 5 to 10 percent on your money these days is a tall order, especially in these times of .5 percent money market funds and 1 percent one-year certificates of deposit. Since making the right investments is beyond the scope of this book, you should meet with the most trusted financial counselor you know, or listen to one that comes highly recommended for offering intelligent investment advice with a proven track record.

I'm not one to pile on guilt here, but a Christian husband has a moral obligation to provide for his family if he unexpectedly dies. Scripture is rather brutal on this topic: "Those who won't care for their relatives, especially those in their own household, have denied the true faith. Such people are worse than unbelievers" (1 Timothy 5:8 NLT).

God gives us that warning through His Word because He doesn't want us to rely on anyone else, or, I suspect, have a church or charity further burdened with another desperate family situation just because the father did not have the foresight to go out and buy some life insurance. Besides, the odds are that the survivors don't have any significant savings to fall back on—otherwise, those credit card bills would be paid off, right?

I realize that there are federal and state government programs providing a "safety net" for widows and their families, and that the US government pays out survivor benefits to families with children younger than eighteen years of age. The average monthly payment for a widow with children under eighteen certainly helps, but it's not a long-range solution to getting a struggling family back on their financial feet.

Despite the creation of Social Security, a husband cannot morally and reasonably expect the government—or the church—to provide more than a partial amount of the money needed to sustain a young family.

You're in Good Hands

Term life insurance—the most popular type of life insurance—is very cheap these days since people are living longer, which means companies can collect premiums longer and pay fewer death benefits. A thirty-five-year-old nonsmoking male, in good health, can purchase $400,000 of term life insurance for $168 per year on a ten-year-level plan, and $500,000 would cost just $195 per year.

If you decide to shop for term life insurance, keep in mind these things:

You need to be in good health. They have a phrase for it: you have to be "insurable" to purchase life insurance. To be insurable, you have to be healthy. Insurance companies won't stay in business very long, for instance, if they take on a new client who has terminal cancer. Insurance companies are also likely to look askance at those who smoke like chimneys, work on power transmission poles for a living, or operate a sky-diving business.

To prove that you are in good health, you will have to submit to a blood test, which allows the insurance company medical staff to screen you for preexisting medical conditions such as diabetes, leukemia, and the HIV virus. If the life insurance company doesn't require one, that's a sure indicator that you will be paying higher rates.

Shop for a ten-year level plan. You can buy term life insurance for one year, ten years, or twenty years, but you must take a blood test each time you start a new policy. That's why annual renewable plans can be tricky, especially after age fifty. Go for the ten-year-level plan, which means the insurance company will sell you a certain amount of life insurance and guarantee the same rate over the life of the commitment— ten years. You pay more in the upfront years, but you make up for that in the back end, which results in a savings of 20 to 25 percent.

A ten-year plan also offers you the flexibility to opt out and start the ten-year clock running all over again in case prices drop—provided you can donate a couple of vials of healthy blood. Just make sure you don't opt out of your present term life insurance until you pass that blood test.

Let's take another hypothetical scenario, but one that is grimmer. Let's say that at the end of your ten-year-level insurance plan, you're shopping for new insurance. A nurse practitioner drops by your home and retrieves a sample of your blood. The laboratory technician, God forbid, discovers that you have prostate cancer. Of course, the new insurance company will not accept you, but you still can stay with your present insurance company because you cannot be canceled, even at the end of your ten-year term. The insurance company will, however, jack up your annual premium (probably times two or three) since they have no idea how healthy you are. But at least you and your family will be covered as you battle the life-threatening cancer.

Insurance You Don't Need

Spending smart means being careful about all your major purchases, and that includes other types of insurance. For instance, you've probably heard that you can't go through life without some form of disability insurance. On its face, disability insurance sounds great—who wouldn't want to be insured in case you lose an eye or become disabled following a car accident? But in my opinion, the rates are too high to replace 60 to 65 percent of your income. If you earn $60,000 a year, you'll have to pay 2 percent of your annual income to be covered, or $100 a month. That's a lot for a policy written with loopholes in favor of the insurance companies.

You probably receive monthly direct-mail letters from your mortgage company offering mortgage life insurance. The pitch goes like this: in the event of your death, the insurance pays off your mortgage, offering you "peace of mind." Actually, this is just another form of term life insurance for the amount of your mortgage, and it's probably not near the eight times of annual income you should be insured for. For instance, a policy that promises to pay off a hefty $250,000 mortgage costs more than $250 a year. You can buy the same amount of term life insurance for $115 on a ten-year-level plan!

Then there are those come-ons for credit card insurance that come in the mail, and they are especially targeted toward those with substantial credit card debt. The prosaic letters promise to pay off your credit card balances in the event of your untimely demise, but like mortgage insurance, these premiums are 50 to 100 percent higher. They are mainly marketed to those who would have trouble qualifying for regular life insurance since they don't require a blood test.

You can also disregard any solicitations for accidental death and "double indemnity" coverage. These policies are no better than shooting craps with the insurance company. What are the chances of dying in a car wreck or plane crash, or smacking a tree while skiing? Very, very low. Accidental death is still a rare occurrence in our modern society.

As for double indemnity coverage, this means that the insurance company will pay double the face value if you die accidentally. If you're the gambler type, then the insurance company wants $200 from you to place the bet.

When it comes to spending smart on insurance, you'll never go wrong by keeping things simple. Seek out adequate term life insurance, skip the exotic and much more expensive death policies, and you'll sleep more soundly.

Isn't that what good life insurance is all about?

13

Giving It the Old College Try

How are we going to pay for college?

This is the question that parents of high school students ask themselves—sometimes in the middle of the night. It doesn't do any good to bellyache about it, but college tuition has risen at more than *double* the increases in the general cost of living in the last twenty years. If you have your heart set on sending Joshua to Harvard next year, the four-year cost will be over $200,000. If he stays close to home, a four-year education at a state school can cost as much as $100,000 when including room and board.

Why so much? Answers are hard to come by, but many parents decided that the more expensive the tuition, the better the degree. Educators caught on to this phenomenon: *Hey, parents are willing to shell out for prestige. They'll pay just about anything.* Thus, the pressure on parents to get their kids into prestigious schools meant tens of thousands of applications for several thousand spots. The law of supply and demand dictated higher and higher tuition rates.

But with a tough job market for college grads and the looming specter of student loans, parents and students are in a tough place. Is a college degree worth $100,000 or more? The answer: it should be. According to the U.S. Census Bureau, college graduates earn far more over their working lifetimes than non–college graduates. The more education you get, the more likely it is that you'll always have a job. Experts say that by the year 2028, there will be 19 million more jobs for educated workers than there are qualified people to fill them.[1] But today's tepid economy has taken some of the luster off that sparkling future.

What concerns me even more is how many of today's college graduates are dealing with an unprecedented amount of student debt. The loan payments, which start six months after graduation, are more than the average car payment and will take decades to pay off. That's a tough way to start a career.

I went to college back in the day when schools weren't asking for the fatted calf—and the rest of the herd—for Jack or Jill to attend an institution of higher learning. Although my out-of-state tuition costs at the University of Oregon stretched my parents, I graduated without owing anyone a nickel. That means during my first few post-college years, I was able to do some fun things, like live and work at a California ski resort, before "settling down." Living in the town of Mammoth Lakes is where I met my future wife, Nicole, who was a visiting ski instructor from Switzerland, and Dr. James Dobson, who owned a vacation condominium in Mammoth. Meeting Dr. Dobson led me to Focus on the Family.

There are no ski bum days ahead for today's college students. As for our two children, Nicole and I were able to put them through Christian college—they both attended Azusa Pacific University in the Los Angeles area—without having any debt hanging over them at graduation. That was a miracle of the Lord's provision in many ways, as well as sacrifices on our part and on our children's, who both worked when they could.

It was worth it, of course, but what was even better was the fact that our children were able to attend a Christ-centered college. Speaking after the fact, I strongly believe that sending children to a Christian college may be the most important decision parents have to make as their children enter young adulthood.

I can remember Dr. Dobson having a big influence in that decision. He said that parents are ultimately responsible for their children's education, and at Christian colleges they were likely to be surrounded by faculty and students with the same Christian worldview—and the students may be more important. "The single greatest influence during the college years does not come from the faculty," he said. "It is derived from other students. Thus, being classmates with men and women who profess a faith in Jesus Christ is vital to the bonding that should occur during those four years."[2]

The benefits—perhaps eternal—of having your son or daughter hanging out with Christian peers and being taught by Christian mentors and role models is crucial during this time of transition. If you're looking for more advice in this area, I highly recommend David Wheaton's book, *The University of Destruction*.[3]

Tip Time

When it comes to navigating the college years, here are some other college-bound strategies to remember:

Shy away from prepaid tuition programs. While plans vary in details, the family pays into a state program a set amount of money each month based on the age of the child. The state then invests the money and guarantees that the child's four-year tuition costs will be paid at any state public institution, regardless of how much tuition rates may rise.

I don't like prepaid plans for several reasons, the biggest being that it takes the option of Christian higher education out of your hands. Family situations change; do you know for sure where you will be living in a decade?

Instead, if you are a disciplined investor, then you can do better investing that monthly amount on your own.

Don't believe the sticker price. Many private universities charge $40,000 and up for one year of tuition and room and board. Yet these same colleges have "endowments" because generous alumni contribute to the old alma mater—especially after a winning football season. At any rate, these endowments enable the college financial aid office to offer a number of "merit grants" to incoming students. This financial aid does not have to be repaid.

A merit grant may be as much as $5,000, even $10,000, which brings out-of-pocket expenses down and may make the difference between you being able to pay as you go instead of borrowing student loan money.

Talk to your son or daughter about your expectations. Anyone who is college-bound should know exactly what he or she is expected to contribute, and you should outline what sacrifices you are willing to make to cover the high cost of college tuition. You may want to reassure these young adults that you'll stick by them.

For instance, when I was growing up, I always heard that college was 50 percent study and 50 percent social. Andrea and Patrick understood early that they were not going to any "party schools" after they graduated from high school. That helped everyone a great deal when it came to discussing what college they were going to attend.

"Gap years" are a luxury. My family was not in favor of "gap years," or taking a year off in the middle of college to explore life or travel. The days of using a gap year to traipse through Europe with a Eurorail pass and a backpack went out with Woodstock. Our goal was to *get in and get out*, and it worked. This was not a harsh policy, but rather a recognition that many college students do not return once they leave school for a year.

Ask them to take advanced placement tests. This was the best thing I did when I was in high school, and it saved my parents and me one year of college. I took AP tests in several subjects, which helped me enter college with thirty credits, or two-thirds of a school year. Even though I had to work hard my last year, averaging eighteen units per semester, I graduated from the University of Oregon in three years and saved my parents a bundle.

Several schools are offering three-year degree programs even if they don't take advanced placement. Check out *College Board Index of Majors and Graduate Degrees* at your library or local bookstore. Drury University in Springfield, Missouri, and Albertus Magnus University in New Haven, Connecticut, offer three-year degrees.

Your children can also earn college credit through the International Baccalaureate program offered at some high schools, and from College-Level Examination Placement (CLEP) tests, a national program that tests for proficiency in several subject areas.

If your kid has talent, push it. If your child is an excellent student, athlete, musician, or actor, then tell your talented teen to look at the extra time spent studying or practicing as a part-time job. Would they rather be practicing their crosscourt backhands or working the fry station at McDonald's? More and more athletic scholarships are available for young women, thanks to Title IX laws.

Consider one of the service academies—army, navy, or air force academies. The competition is strong, but cadets at one of the US service academies receive tuition, room and board, and a monthly stipend while incurring a commitment to serve in the military for a number of years—usually six—after graduation.

Take a video tour of the college. Sure, you'll want to personally visit your child's top choice or two, but you can whittle down your options by going on YouTube and looking at video tours.

Don't seek early admission. If your child decides early, you can't play off one college's financial aid or scholarship program against another.

Ask the kids to attend a community college for a year or two. Tuition fees are not only lower, but you can save money by having your college student live at home. Use that savings to fund the final two years at an out-of-town school.

If you have a local state university, having your son or daughter remain at home saves a lot on room and board. This may not be the ideal situation, of course, since the college experience involves cutting the so-called "apron strings" from Mom and Dad. If this is important to your child, perhaps a compromise can be struck by agreeing to finance the last year or two at an out-of-town university.

Parents often debate the pros and cons of deciding in favor of a local college. If your son or daughter remains at home, remember that he or she will probably need a car, which can cost several thousand dollars a year. At an out-of-town university, most students who live on campus can get by with just a bike. (I never had a car during college, so there!)

Ask the kids to work. That's what our kids did, although Andrea couldn't work very much because she was on the Azusa Pacific tennis team. If earning several thousand dollars a year is the difference between taking on college loans or graduating from college debt-free, then work is a good thing. Your kids will also appreciate their education more and learn the value of gainful employment.

Somehow, by hook or by crook, get them through without incurring debt. If your spouse has to take on a full-time job or if you have to work overtime, or if your student has to participate in a work-study program, that's the way it will be.

If you have to get a loan, do everything you can to pay it off before graduation. The worse-case scenario is taking out a home-equity loan or refinancing your mortgage, since that will be a financial setback. Borrowing against your retirement plan is another option, although there could be a major tax penalty. Some retirement plans allow you to borrow your pre-tax dollars as long as you repay in a certain time period—usually five years.

Encourage summer school. If tuition is cheaper during the summer, why not go? And what about taking summer classes at your community college? Just make sure credits are transferable.

Encourage summer internships. Interns may work for peanuts, but it's a great way to make contacts for that first post-college job.

Finally, keep in mind that paying for college is a daunting prospect, but it has been done. Just remember to give it the "old college try."

Checkout Lane

Have you ever lived next door to trashy neighbors?

You know, the family who parks their broken-down cars on the street, lets the lawn grow into a jungle of knee-high weeds, and lives in such a filthy house that you ban your kids from stepping inside the front door?

Then one Saturday morning, you notice the father mowing the grass and his two teenage boys pulling weeds in the flower garden. That's the first time you've seen them working in the yard all summer. But they don't stop there. They rake up the remaining clumps of grass and spread seed and fertilizer across the blotchy expanse.

Meanwhile, work crews have shown up. One crew preps the outside of the house for painting while other workers overhaul inside the house, which appears to be a beehive of remodeling activity. The house is also getting a new kitchen.

Over the next six weeks, the house undergoes a dramatic transformation. The junky cars are towed away, the driveway is resurfaced, the kitchen is redone, and the house receives a fresh coat of paint from top to bottom, inside and out. Then, after the last work crew has left, the family plants a FOR SALE sign in the lush, green grass.

You shake your head in disbelief. With a little effort, your neighbors could have gotten their house in tip-top shape long ago.

The same thought applies to our finances. Couples who spend smartly and wisely have their financial house in order and are better positioned to deal with life's unexpected turns. I hope I've inspired you to think about ways you can save money on household items or make better big-ticket purchases.

Let me close with this thought: the reason I try to spend smartly and wisely is so that Nicole and I have more resources to support the Lord's work. We enjoy providing for our local church, various missionaries we've gotten to know over the years, and our Compassion International and World Vision children.

There's freedom in spending smartly—freedom from debt, freedom from overspending, freedom from having too much stuff.

The greatest freedom comes from knowing that we have the freedom to give.

Source Materials

Chapter 2: Gimme Credit

1. "Indebted U.S. Household Carrying More Than $15,000 in Credit Card Debt," Cornerstone Credit Union League, April 8, 2014, http://www.cornerstoneleague.coop /indebted_u_s_household_carrying_more_than_15_000_ in_credit_card_debt.html.

2. Ramsey, Dave. *The Total Money makeover: A Proven Plan for Financial Fitness* (Nashville: Thomas Nelson, 2003), 31.

3. Danielle Kurtzleben. "CHARTS: Americans Increasingly Paying Off Their Credit Cards," *U.S. News*, December 17, 2013, http://www.usnews.com/news/ articles/2013/12/17/charts-americans-increasingly-paying -off-their-credit-cards.

Chapter 4: Supermarket Sweep

1. Hitt, Jack. "The Theory of Supermarkets," *New York Magazine*, March 10, 1996.

2. "Guess How Many Items the Average Grocery Shopper Buys in a Year?" *Coupons in the News*, January 23, 2014, http://couponsinthenews.com/2014/01/23/guess-how -many-items-the-average-grocery-shopper-buys-in-a-year/.

Chapter 6: Let's Go Out for a Bite to Eat

1. Hudson Riehle. "Restaurant Technology: Critical for Tomorrow's Success," National Restaurant Association, October 24, 2013, http://www.restaurant.org/Downloads /PDFs/NetworkingGroups/RIS-Restaurant-Technology -Presentation-by-Hudson-R.pdf.

Chapter 11: Why Gambling Is a Bad Bet

1. Elise Young and Alex McIntyre. "Georgia Lottery Players Suckers Spending Most for Least," *Bloomberg*, March 14, 2012, http://www.bloomberg.com/news/2012 -03-14/georgia-lottery-players-suckers-spending-most-for -least.html.

2. Larry Light. "How Gambling Is Snookering America," book review of Timothy L. O'Brien's *Bad Bet: The Inside Story of the Glamour, Glitz, and Danger of America's Gambling Industry*, *Business Week*, November 9, 1998, http:// www.businessweek.com/1998/45/b3603087.htm.

3. Read more at Got Questions.org., http://www .gotquestions.org/gambling-sin.html. Adapted from "Is Gambling a Sin?" (Got Questions Ministries, 2002–14).

Chapter 13: Giving It the Old College Try

1. "College Graduates Earn More," Lorain Community College (Elyria, OH), accessed September 25, 2014, https://lorainccc.edu/future+students/college+graduates+earn+more.htm.

2. From Mike Yorkey, *Saving Money Any Way You Can* (Ann Arbor, MI: Servant, 1994), 221.

3. David Wheaton, *The University of Destruction: Your Game Plan for Spiritual Victory on Campus* (Minneapolis: Bethany House, 2005).

About the Author

Mike Yorkey, a veteran writer, is the author or coauthor of more than eighty-five books with more than 2 million copies in print. He has collaborated with Tampa Bay Rays' Ben Zobrist and his wife, Julianna, a Christian music artist, in *Double Play*; Cleveland Browns quarterback Colt McCoy and his father, Brad, in *Growing Up Colt*; San Francisco Giants pitcher Dave Dravecky in *Called Up*; San Diego Chargers placekicker Rolf Benirschke in *Alive & Kicking*; tennis star Michael Chang in *Holding Serve*; and Rutgers defensive tackle Eric LeGrand in *Believe: My Faith and the Tackle That Changed My Life*.

Mike is also the coauthor of the internationally bestselling Every Man's Battle series with Steve Arterburn and Fred Stoker, and his latest book is *Light the Way Home* with KKLA radio talk show host Frank Sontag (www.franksontag.net).

He and his wife, Nicole, are the parents of two adult children and make their home in Encinitas, California.

Mike's website is www.mikeyorkey.com.

Notes